Supporting Special Educational Needs in Secondary School Classrooms

Jane Lovey

David Fulton Publishers
London

Published in association with the Roehampton Institute

David Fulton Publishers Ltd
2 Barbon Close, London WC1N 3JX

First published in Great Britain by
David Fulton Publishers 1995

Note: The right of Jane Lovey to be identified as the author of this work has been asserted by her in accordance with the Copyright, Designs and Patents Act 1988.

Copyright © Jane Lovey

British Library Cataloguing in Publication Data

A catalogue record for this book is available from the British Library

ISBN 1-85346-339-6

Typeset by RP Typesetters Ltd., Unit 13, 21 Wren Street, London WC1X 0HF.

Printed in Great Britain by BPC Books & Journals Ltd, Exeter.

Contents

ACKNOWLEDGEMENTS

I would like to offer my sincere thanks to Jim Docking whose very generous help while editing this book was invaluable to me.

I would also like to express my gratitude to all my professional colleagues, and to my pupils and their parents who gave their valuable time to help me by sharing their ideas about support with me.

Introduction

During the last decade the support teacher for children with special educational needs has become an essential member of staff in most schools. Such teachers sit alongside children in mainstream classrooms and help them, or withdraw them for extra help, whilst making sure they are aware of the expectations of their subject teacher.

There is no shortage of accounts in journal articles and books about the work of the support teacher. Much is written about the liaison that should ideally take place regularly between classteachers and support teachers, with advice on joint planning and sharing the lesson. However, little appears to have been written about the day-to-day realities of support in the secondary school classroom. In some schools, it might be possible to produce the ideal model described in the literature. Unfortunately, in many schools, however willing staff are to give children with special needs the fairest possible access to the curriculum, there are not the resources to meet these standards.

This book is concerned with the realities of support in the secondary school as we know it as well as how it might ideally exist. The focus is on secondary schools rather than schools in general because there are very different approaches and skills needed when supporting pupils who move from teacher to teacher throughout the school day. In the higher forms of a secondary school there is the question of whether a non-specialist can effectively help children with their work in a specialised subject. The author's experience is of being a peripatetic support teacher for statemented pupils with many different needs in nine secondary schools in one London Borough. The advice and experience of other support teachers based in individual schools has been invaluable in producing this book.

A recent research project was set up to identify indicators of effective support in secondary schools (Lovey 1993). In this study the views of parents and children, as well as their specialist and support teachers and headteachers, were collected (details in Chapter 8). What emerged was a scenario in which the prevailing commitment to provide effective support was frustrated by the means by which resources are allocated to schools. Because funding is allocated to pupils on a termly or annual basis, schools are unable to offer their support staff any degree of job security. The creation of a centrally funded post in the Borough was an attempt to solve the problem of providing appropriate support quickly, but this resulted in both time and money being spent in travelling from school to school. The problems of putting the support where it was needed whilst fitting in time in up to nine schools meant that compromises were often made at the expense of effectiveness. As a result of more of the schools wishing to manage a larger part of their own budgets, the post was discontinued in order to release the funding for delegation to the schools.

It is now over a decade since Fergusson and Adams (1983) warned that it was unlikely that two teachers would be equal partners in the classroom, even though their researchers' observations were based on work in the primary school where there is not the same problem of teacher specialisation as there is in secondary schools. More recently two teacher trainers – Ron Best (1991) and Gary Thomas (1993) – have reported their experience on their 'recent and relevant' teaching as support teachers. Both found that there were many frustrations in this experience. Examples were the lack of opportunity to liaise with the teachers in whose classrooms they were working. However there were occasions when liaison took place but what had been agreed seemed to have been forgotten by the next lesson and planned strategies went by the board. There were also occasions when, had the support teacher just known about a special activity that the subject teacher had planned he could have supervised half the class and enriched the experience for all the children, but, instead, he found himself walking around with the teacher whilst the children wandered around fairly aimlessly, asking each other what they should be doing.

By the beginning of the 1990s much of the optimism and determination for the integration of children with special educational needs into mainstream classrooms had been lost in every school's eagerness for a favourable place in the league tables. Some schools did not want to be renowned for having strategies for supporting these children lest a majority of the children with special needs be directed to them at secondary school transfer.

During the 1980s training in special needs had been priority for government funding. However, by the nineties the emphasis was on teachers becoming experts in their specialism, and appointments to posts which required special needs expertise rather than specialised subject knowledge became fewer. Even when the appointment of a special needs co-ordinator (SENCO) is made, the subject that he or she can offer for specialist teaching is often more important to the appointment committee than a special needs qualification or experience in working with children who have special educational needs. To be fair, it is important that the SENCO in a school does have credibility as a teacher, and this can certainly best be gained by having a regular commitment to teaching a subject in the curriculum. However, given that the job of a SENCO makes great demands on time if all children with special needs and their teachers are to be effectively supported, the combination of subject teaching and SEN co-ordination is often not a sensible proposition.

This book is an attempt to share some of the strategies that effective support teachers use in helping pupils in the classroom in both ideal situations and in those that fall short of the ideal. It is not an attempt to criticise the teachers in whose rooms it is sometimes more difficult to function. Most teachers are eager to serve all the pupils in their care but have a different agenda from the special needs specialist. There are some teachers who find it extremely difficult to empathise with the difficulties of the child who never seems to understand certain concepts, or the child who understands the concepts well but cannot express them satisfactorily. Those teachers, however, are very important for those children at the other end of the SEN continuum, who need an extended curriculum. We cannot ignore the needs of gifted children whose requirements, although special, are often best served by teachers who demand of themselves and pupils the highest of academic standards.

It is to be hoped that sufficient resources will be available to implement the Code of Practice for the Identification and Assessment of Special Educational Needs (DfE 1994). If needs are identified earlier and support is offered as soon as there are difficulties, more children may well be helped before they become so frustrated by failure that they develop the avoidance strategies with which we are all familiar in the classroom.

Throughout my research I found parents were eager to be heard and regretted that it had taken so long to recognise their children's needs. This underlines the importance of involving parents in providing information for the first stage of the assessment process and informing them of decisions which have been made and strategies which are being used to help their child. It is to be hoped that if they are involved from the beginning of the process problems will be solved more quickly. There is no doubt that support will be needed in the classroom from Stage Two when the Individual Educational Plan (IEP) is drawn up. It may well be the support teacher who co-ordinates this under the aegis of the Special Needs Co-ordinator. The role of a well qualified and well supported SENCO will be pivotal in the successful implementation of the Code of Practice.

CHAPTER 1
Always a Bridesmaid, Never the Bride!

The decision that as many children as possible with special educational needs should be given equal access to the curriculum in mainstream schools has without doubt been one of the success stories of the last decade. Young people who would have spent their whole school careers in a very segregated and limited setting have had the opportunity of increased integration with their peers. This would not have been possible without special arrangements having been made in mainstream schools. In some cases it has meant an adaptation of stairs and entrances and the provision of special toilet facilities. With nearly all children with statements it has meant the presence of a second adult in the classroom for at least some of the time.

Non-teaching Classroom Assistants

A distinction needs to be made between classroom assistants and support teachers. In the case where the child has physical difficulties, a non-teaching assistant is often employed for a large part of the timetable. (For simplicity I shall refer to classroom assistants and support teachers as female, as the majority are women. This does not discount the excellent work done by the dedicated minority of men in this role.) She is often largely concerned with necessary hygiene arrangements and movement around the school. Although she is not officially a teacher, she is sometimes an invaluable aide in lessons to provide a steadying hand in a science or technology practical, and to boost the confidence and self-esteem of the pupil who is struggling during the early days of integration. In the primary school the assistant can have an important role for all the children in the class, and the benefits of a second regular adult involved in the class will often offset any anxiety felt by the presence of a disabled child (Swan 1984).

The role of the classroom assistant is much more difficult in the secondary school. With a much larger staff, comprising more specialists and part-timers, it is more difficult for the assistant to have close working links with all the teachers who are responsible for her protégée. It is unlikely that all the teachers in whose classrooms she spends some of her time will regard it as a priority to have regular liaison with her. Often it will only be when there is a problem with the child fitting in with the lesson that a meeting will be sought.

An excellent account of the role of classroom assistants is provided in *Help in the Classroom* by Margaret Balshaw (1993). This is an invaluable handbook for both classroom assistants and the teachers in whose rooms they work.

Support teachers are different from classroom assistants in that they are qualified teachers. As well as teachers who are employed specifically to provide support, there are teachers who support special needs during periods when they are not timetabled to teach their subject.

Support Teachers

The status of the support teacher

A. I've never taken a class but I'm allowed to let them in now. I've even got my own key. I got fed up with lining up with the children, especially if the teacher was late.

B. Oh, we're not allowed to let them in. The teachers are quite definite about that. They say we're not covered by any kind of insurance to do that. We stand in the queue with the children.

C. Yes. I wait for lessons to begin now. It means that when I get in I have to find out what they are doing and of course, some of the children shout out 'Hi miss'.

A. Yes and at the end of the lesson you find yourself standing up behind the chair with the kids, waiting to be dismissed.

C. Yes. Stand up everyone, and up I get. I don't know sometimes whether I am a child or a teacher.

The above conversation was recorded at an INSET session for support teachers employed by secondary schools. All three of the teachers speaking were experienced teachers who had become part-time support teachers following a career break to care for their own young families. One of them had been head of a P.E. department in a tough inner-city secondary school. The other two had been primary school teachers with total responsibility for their classes for a number of years. As can be appreciated from their statements, there was a feeling among them of frustration that their perceived lack of status stood in the way of their effectiveness.

All felt that the children regarded them as 'not quite real teachers'. As a support teacher myself, with nearly thirty years experience behind me, half of that time in very responsible posts, I have been asked, 'Aren't you a bit old to be a student, miss?' and 'Are you Mr D's mum, miss, are you just helping him today?' Three men on the course, all retired from posts of responsibility said they did not feel status was a problem. However, they all admitted to having made it quite clear to the pupils that they had held responsible positions before. One of the men felt that the fact that he helped with sport after school confirmed the fact that he was a 'real teacher'. Another man, reflecting on the status problem, suggested that the fact he roamed round during lesson times, looking for children and carrying a clipboard, could lead some people to think he was a deputy head!

When does our perceived lack of status affect our authority with pupils? I think teacher A's experience is only too typical of what can happen:

...I had a girl this morning who insisted on putting an apostrophe before every 's'. I told her she didn't need them but she said she wanted them there and I couldn't get her to change her mind. The teacher came up and said 'What have you got an apostrophe there for Lisa?' and she immediately rubbed it out. The teacher looked at me reproachfully and I felt that high (putting thumb and fore-finger close together).

Her colleague immediately added:

That's happened to me and I've been humiliated because it just looks as if you've sat there and let the boy do what he likes...and all that you do has to be in *sotto voce.*

Others spoke of the experience of the subject teacher turning round from the board and demanding to know who was talking and having to own up to this charge of disruption whilst they were interpreting to their protégée the work on the board.

Despite its frustrations, the role in which one feels neither child nor adult can be a very valuable learning experience for the teacher interested in observing how learning does (or does not) take place. From our position in the class, the dynamics of the group are exposed in a way in which they are not from the front of the class. The support teachers interviewed told me that they had experienced momentary hurt feelings when they felt that they were being censured for legitimately talking in class. What do we do when our pupils, and others who ask for our help, are reprimanded for talking to us during the lesson? As teachers we can identify with the feelings of the teacher who has an agenda to complete during that lesson. We know from experience how difficult it is to teach when there is a constant undercurrent of conversation. Pupils, without this insight, see the proximity of a second teacher sitting amongst them as an invitation to ask questions that they often do not have the chance or courage to ask the subject teacher. They too must feel hurt when reprimanded for talking to the teacher who is there to support their needs. How can we defend their needs without seeming to criticise or undermine the authority of the teacher? Our loyalties are unavoidably divided between our professional colleagues and the pupils whose advocates we need to be.

This could be a powerful and useful position for both teachers, were not most support teachers so sensitive to their position as guest of the teacher in whose room they carry out their work. Information from the support teacher about the reaction of the average and below-average pupils sitting in the class can be invaluable for the class-teacher in planning the next lesson. In some classes this is precisely what happens and is indeed encouraged, but often the relationship between the two teachers is too delicate for the guest to make any comment that might sound like criticism. Instead she feels she has to wait patiently until the host teacher feels secure enough to reflect on the lesson with her.

Censure of bad behaviour in class is another problem for support teachers. It is absolutely necessary to attend the class a few times before attempting to intervene in matters of discipline as individual teachers work with different levels of noise and interruption. Nevertheless, sometimes a quiet word in the ear of a child who is misbehaving nearby can pre-empt and be more effective than a humiliating public reprimand by the subject teacher from the front of the class. All the support teachers who were interviewed found it difficult to decide to what extent they should reprimand a pupil when they were not in charge of the class. When asked what action they would like support teachers to take in keeping class order, some subject teachers became very concerned and asked that all misdemeanours should be reported to them so that they could deal with them. There was a consensus of opinion that teachers often saw any discussion on discipline as a suggestion that they were not doing their job properly in controlling the class: perhaps they were afraid this was the message that pupils would get. Unless or until the support teacher is accepted very much as a partner and ally of the subject teacher, it is probably safer to rely on the quiet preventative word, the finger on the lips, the raised eyebrow or other universal admonitory gestures, and only discuss class management if the subject is introduced by the specialist teacher.

In most situations the support teacher is better not to be seen to be taking any kind of lead in the lesson, whatever his or her previous responsibility and skills. Such intervention could be counter-productive if the class perceive it as a symptom of the subject teacher's incompetence. There are, however, situations where the skill and experience of both teachers can be exploited to the full for the good of the children. This is assuming there is enough time for the kind of consultation and collaboration which leads to a real classroom partnership.

The aims of support in the classroom

One of the primary aims of the support teacher is to enable children who would otherwise be segregated to take their place in mainstream. However in the secondary school such support is not easy to organise. On a statement of SEN, for instance, the main recommendation is often for the child to have a structured programme of support to improve literacy skills. Subject teachers, however, have very definite ideas about the specific piece of work they want the support teacher to help the pupil to complete. In some cases, such as in the writing up of a science experiment or the completing of a geography worksheet, this piece of work may present little opportunity to address literacy difficulties. Sometimes the concepts needed to understand that piece of work are beyond the child who is being supported. Obviously this means that more time should be spent in prior liaison between subject and support teachers so that support which addresses the literacy problem can be properly planned.

However, this is easier said than done, everyone familiar with secondary schools knows how little time there is for regular liaison about individual pupils. There is also the problem that support teachers are funded only for the time they are in the classroom with the child. Few schools budget extra money to enable liaison to take place during non-contact time when matters such as literacy skills could be attended to. It is also not possible to adapt the timetable of a large secondary school to fit in with the specific support needs of each individual pupil.

So given these practical constraints, what realistically can support aim to achieve? To begin with, a need of nearly every statemented pupil is the development of self-esteem. Help in completing a good piece of work and subsequent self-evaluation can add to this in many ways. In a lesson taught from the front, it is often possible for the support teacher to anticipate the questions which will be asked and judiciously to arm one's protégée with some of the answers so that he or she can at least have the satisfaction of providing the right answers some of the time. If the class is engaged in a project the support teacher can often provide some extra component for this that the child can share with his classmates. Another factor in relation to self-esteem is that the pupil(s) have the opportunity to talk through what they are doing with an adult and so are helped to remember the lesson. Indeed talking things through can be extended by encouraging peer help. Those children most in need of help are often very good at referring themselves to the support teacher. They can form a group within the classroom in which the children will continue to help each other and work things out even when the support teacher is not there, especially if they know she will be interested to know what they have done on her next visit. In the next chapter, the issue of enhancing self-esteem will be developed further.

When the aim of the lesson is not linked to the needs described in the statement, another way in which effective support can be given, is by mediating the learning. Able and confident children often experiment and think out aloud when searching for solutions to problems. They are dogged in their pursuit of a solution. For a number of reasons, such as their wider vocabulary and their more effortless use of language, or the culture and ethos of their home environment, they often have better developed thinking skills than their lower achieving classmates. However, thinking skills can be taught to children who are deficient in them. The work of Bloom (1956), de Bono (1970), Feuerstein (1980), Lipman (1980) and Blagg (1988) makes convincing claims about how the performance of below-average pupils can be greatly enhanced by a systematic programme of thinking skills.

One of the important aspects of encouraging thinking skills which is advocated by Feuerstein (1980) is in mediating a child's experience or learning. We do this when we talk to him about his learning and examine aloud the processes we are going through in our thinking about a subject. For instance, in a technology lesson the child might have been asked to make a small container from wood. How will he do this? What is the function of the container? Why has wood been chosen as the material? Recall similar containers with which we are familiar. Which ones are effective in their aim and which fall short of their function? Any number of questions can be pondered whilst preparing to commence the task. It is important that the child develops the habit of adopting this style of thinking.

The presence of the support teacher in such a lesson can make it a stimulating experience which will have an effect in other lessons. This should help to minimise the occasions when the child spends much of the lesson talking to others socially whilst awaiting a turn on the lathe, or the subject teacher's attention. When a pupil has struggled through his thinking to reach a conclusion, the support teacher can help him to reflect on how his point was reached. This process can be part of almost every lesson or task. More will be said about developing thinking skills in Chapter 3 in the section 'Thinking about thinking'.

The partnership with subject teachers

Much has been said about partnership or collaboration in the class-room by those who wrote the early literature on support. Thomas (1992) started his book on classroom teams with a section on the importance of selecting a team carefully to ensure balance. However when he relates his actual experience of working as a support teacher in a secondary school, he writes of frustrations and misunderstandings. Bell and Best (1986) produced one of the most encouraging and influential accounts of good practice in support in secondary schools. I have no reason to doubt that the initiatives of which they write were in place in the early 1980s in some schools. It is valuable to record examples of good practice, and therefore anyone preparing a work on support would be justified in recording only those instances where it was successful. There would be little point in this context to cite examples which were not effective. However, like Thomas, Best (1991) later provided a very honest account of how it was when he did some work as a support teacher in a secondary school, revealing how the realities of the situation could jeopardise effective support.

That the presence of a second teacher in the classroom does not automatically lead to a collaborative partnership is not altogether surprising. In many ways a teacher who is employed not to teach, but to sit in the classroom among the children, is an anomaly. Teachers are trained to take a lead in their classroom. One of the main roles of a good teacher is to be an efficient classroom manager. This means controlling and teaching a large group of young people. In the secondary school the subject teacher will also have loyalty to the faculty, which makes the delivery of a specialist subject in a professional way of paramount importance. Although the presence in the classroom of another person sitting quietly and helping a struggling youngster is an undeniable help, that person is not necessarily seen by the subject teacher as a partner in the classroom. Those who describe a true partnership in the classroom – where subject and support teachers take turns in leading the lesson – are usually describing a very different situation, and are often talking about the primary school.

In order to produce a true partnership in secondary school classrooms, it would be necessary to:

- employ specialist subject support teachers, not generalists;
- meet for liaison before every lesson;
- have the resources for far more pupil support than is usual at present.

It is encouraging to note that some subject teachers who have received their initial teacher training since the advent of support teachers in the classroom have seemed much more willing to work in a genuinely collaborative way with support teachers.

How then can subject and support teachers realistically liaise to improve the quality of pupil support? One of the most useful collaborative activities is in looking together at textbooks and worksheets and either adapting them to make them accessible by the whole class or producing an alternative version for members of the class with special needs.

The latter strategy raises one of the most vexed questions concerning differentiation in the classroom, namely whether giving out different worksheets is effectively a form of streaming and whether it therefore stigmatises certain pupils. Some teachers are not comfortable with the distribution of different materials, claiming that effective differentiation occurs in the way the pupil is helped to do the work. There is a validity in this claim provided that two important conditions are met. The first is that the worksheets are designed in such a way that they can easily be read by all those with a reading age of 7+ (unless it is known that a support teacher is going to be available for poor readers). The second condition is that the outcome is open-ended enough not to leave any pupil feeling helpless and frustrated. The danger in providing just one version of such a worksheet for a whole class is that some pupils may be insufficiently challenged, whilst others might constantly experience the humiliation of never completing a worksheet.

There are often several children in a class who could better demonstrate what they have learned by using an adapted worksheet. After all if we have a partially sighted child in the class we would provide either large print or Braille. It is unlikely that the classmates of a child in need of support are not already aware of his difficulties and sympathetic to them. By extension, there should be no ethical or motivational obstacle to providing differentiated worksheets for children with learning difficulties. However, it is the teacher who sits in the class among the pupils who is best able to say what form of differentiation will be most suitable in that setting. More will be said about this in later chapters.

Unless the support teacher happens to be a specialist in the subject, it is unlikely there would be any advantage in him or her leading some of the lessons. The situation is quite different, however, in cases where the support teacher has relevant subject expertise. It is unfortunate that often support teachers seem to lack the confidence to claim their specialism. For instance, if the support teacher is a modern language specialist, the presence of a second specialist enabling two oral groups to be formed and giving children the opportunity of hearing two adults communicate in the target language is clearly a great advantage. There might also be sections of a geography or history syllabus where the support teacher could usefully take the lead because he or she has had firsthand knowledge of the country or event under discussion. A retired headteacher whom I know regularly leads sessions on the D–Day invasion and brings in Second World War memorabilia even though he is not a history specialist. His vivid input to the lesson, based on his personal experience, led a record number of boys to sign up for the Normandy Beaches trip during one half-term.

What now of the problem of misbehaviour in the context of a partnership? Although discipline is often a delicate subject between the subject teacher and the support teacher, some partners work out a system which can cut down on unnecessary interruptions to the lesson and recognise children whose behaviour is worthy of positive comment. For example, a quiet move by the support teacher over to a child who is talking or providing other distractions is often enough to stop the disruption going further and to put the child back on task. Again, because of the support teacher's position as a regular member of staff, sitting among the pupils, a child can often be returned to work by offering help in the current activity or referring back to something the child did well on a previous occasion. The support teacher can also quickly answer the questions of the small band of pupils who find it difficult to start a piece of work without a great deal of reassurance from the teacher. Although these children are often quiet and hard-working, in a large class their need for help at the beginning of every task can provide cover for the more disruptive elements to delay engagement in any kind of work. Again, a support teacher can often deal with potentially confrontational situations, such as lending a pen or pencil to the child who has forgotten, broken or lost his or her equipment. This means the child can start work straight away, so avoiding the usual censure for coming to class without the right tools. Later, when reclaiming the pen or pencil, the support teacher can quietly discuss why a pen was not brought and suggest strategies for making sure that this does not happen again.

If the subject teacher and the support teacher can occasionally find time to sit down together and reflect on how their interaction in the class is affecting the pupils, this can help greatly in planning differentiation of input and outcome. This has happened successfully in a large, mixed-ability first year class who were learning to read grid-references on Ordnance Survey maps. It was agreed that as the abler children finished, the subject teacher would go to them with the next stage of the exercise. Meanwhile, as the support teacher, I would monitor the progress of the 'strugglers', including two children who were statemented because of moderate learning difficulties. I was able to give them further practice in the process with which they were struggling, until they gained confidence in finding four figure references with no help. Had they felt compelled to keep up with the rest of the class they would not have internalised the basic concept on which they were able to build in later lessons. In this class there were a few children who, while not having serious learning difficulties, lacked confidence when faced with new work. They often asked for my help in reinforcing basic concepts before going on to the next stage with the class-teacher. This is an effective way to work in any lesson where the two teachers can be prepared to cater for the different needs. Children with transient learning difficulties are usually quick to refer themselves in this kind of non-threatening learning environment.

A very important agreement for the two teachers to make concerns the occasions pupils might be allowed to leave the room to go to the lavatory. It is obviously not a partnership if the support teacher has to refer the child to the other teacher for every such request, but equally it is important that children who have been refused permission by one should not immediately go to the other teacher and gain permission! Policies to pre-empt situations of this kind are an important aspect of any partnership between specialist and support teacher.

The receptive and reflective role of the support teacher

Because the support teacher rarely has any control over the agenda in the classroom, and often has not been present at the previous lesson, she has to be immediately receptive to the content and aims of the lesson. Within minutes, pupils can be asking for help and reassurance in a subject of which the support teacher has little knowledge. To keep approaching the subject teacher for advice would clearly be disruptive, so it is important that the support teacher has read the textbook in advance of the lesson. This is not easily achieved in schools where textbooks are at a premium and not allowed to be taken out of the classroom or laboratory. Although the support teacher may be distracted by the behaviour of the children nearby, and sitting on a too small chair in an irritating draught, the result of missing anything the subject teacher says at the beginning of the lesson could be the humiliation of having helped pupils to do the wrong thing!

It is also important to be sensitive to the mood of the pupils being helped. This is especially important when the reason for the statement is emotional or behavioural difficulties. With adolescents it is important to be able to read their body language and match yours to it (Lovey 1992, Chapter 7). There are days when every inch of the young person indicates anger. This is often not the time when he or she can be humoured into producing the work. It might be the day to bide your time and help the pupil to avoid confrontation with the teacher which would happen if the anger were to boil over. It might be appropriate to concentrate on getting the work headed up so that when the pupil accepts the inevitability of having to conform to the demands of the lesson an encouraging start has been made. If the child is preoccupied with his or her own concerns, help that normally would be seen as inappropriate in a lesson might have to be given. *How to Cope with Childhood Stress: A practical guide for teachers* (Alsop and McCaffrey 1993) provides a useful insight into the problems with which many children cope. After all, this is all part of achieving the aim to keep this troubled young person integrated in the mainstream. The receptive support teacher will adapt his or her style to fit the needs of both teacher and pupil even if this sometimes means making compromises.

There are times when I have been supporting a seriously stressed pupil in a lesson where there has been a requirement to produce notes on a science experiment. I have printed a heading and date, and pencilled in a very basic diagram. If refusal to co-operate has continued, I have written the notes leaving gaps to insert the key words. These words I have written on a scrap of paper for when the time is right for the pupil to complete the work. This is not spoon-feeding. Rather it can break the pattern of failure experienced by these pupils with recurring preoccupations from their chaotic lives outside the classroom, who find, when they have to attempt to revise for a test, that they have discouraging gaps in their books. This is another special strategy that recognises that emotional difficulties can be as disabling as learning or sensory difficulties. As support teachers, we have to look carefully at the aims of the statement and match the intention to the manifest needs of the child.

There can be few support teachers who, at the end of the day, do not reflect on their input. Unlike other teachers who are so busy preparing lessons for the next day, our preparation load is comparatively manageable. However, since much of what we do is a reaction to the situation in which we find ourselves, there is always the question of what we would have done had we had opportunity to prepare for the event. The group of support teachers whose conversations I recorded often had difficulty in knowing why they were as undoubtedly effective as they were:

A. ...I was told by a mother that just my presence there had made a difference to her son, even if I was not doing anything. I don't know. I'll accept that. The child started to work hard and still is. I didn't think I had done all that much. The SENCO asked me what I had done. I said, 'Not much' but the boy is off statement and coping fine now.

B. You obviously boosted his self-esteem. That's important.

C. The kids recognise we help them. The other kids also like you going in.

B. I wonder if it is because we talk to them. In the course of a week a child is rarely spoken to individually by a teacher.

C. I can think of two children I had. I don't know what I did but I know that having my support stopped them from truanting. People said that they would definitely have gone off the rails if I hadn't been there a couple of times a week for them.

A. It all comes down to the fact that you care and you show the children that.

(I had some reservations about including the last comment as there is no doubt that the majority of secondary school teachers do care a great deal about their individual pupils, but have less opportunity to show this.)

This exchange of views sums up secondary support in many ways:

- the SEN child has a teacher/advocate/ally in the classroom;
- the SEN child has easy access to help and reassurance;
- the support teacher can concentrate on responding positively to the SEN child's achievements and so build up his or her self-esteem;
- the support teacher is in the position of being able to have a quiet word with a child before a threatened confrontation;
- the disaffected child knows that there is someone who will notice what he or she does;
- a second teacher means all the children have more attention.

By regularly making an effort to reflect on the aims of the support given, the perceptions of individual children to their situation, and the nature of his learning difficulties, a better attempt can be made to match support to the needs.

The importance of the statement of special educational needs and individual educational plans

The most important instrument in matching support to the needs is the well written statement. It is essential that the support teacher knows what is actually written on the statement about the specific needs of each child supported. It is difficult to deliver individual programmes in the secondary school, but there is now a need to overcome this difficulty for *all* children with special needs, not just those with statements. Since the introduction of the Code of Practice (DfE 1994), many children who, we hope, will never reach the stage of being statemented, will be on Individual Educational Plans.

The Code of Practice is discussed more fully in Chapter 8. This document recommends five stages for the identification and assessment of special needs. The first stage involves the child's teachers, with the help of the SENCO, using their own strategies to try to alleviate the child's problems. Stages Two and Three involve the making of an Individual Educational Plan (IEP) for the child. At Stage Two this will be drawn up by the SENCO, but at Stage Three the support of specialist support teams, or the educational psychologist, will assist in drawing up this Plan. Stage Four, where the LEA is

involved, will not be embarked upon until the IEP has been monitored and assessed through at least two reviews. Stage Five is the
point at which a Statement of Special Needs is produced.

Support from Sixth Form pupils

In schools where there is a Sixth Form, some of these young men
and women can provide a very special kind of support for younger
pupils. However, support by sixth formers should not be seen as an
economy but be an exercise that is as beneficial to the sixth former
as the pupil receiving this special kind of support. Supporting
younger pupils in lessons of their own specialist subjects can help
sixth formers to develop greater understanding of some of the
concepts that they have grasped easily and taken for granted. Support
of younger pupils is also invaluable experience for helping sixth
formers to make decisions about whether they wish to train as
teachers. However, if the sixth formers are recruited to help they
should be supported by a teacher with a specialism in special needs.
Details of different kinds of support given by sixth formers will be
described in future chapters.

The special skills of the support teacher

The role of the support teacher is by its very nature a subsidiary one.
However it is one that requires a great deal of reflective and negotia-
tional skills, skills which might not often be required together.
Although support teachers do not enjoy the overtly powerful role of
the class-teacher, they have a vital role as an advocate for the individual pupil with whom they work. The potential of support teachers
for making the individual child's time in school effective is unrivalled. The next chapter will deal with one of the most important
aspects of this role – that of being the person in the best position to
make the special child, and sometimes his or her teacher, feel good.

CHAPTER 2
Classroom support and self-esteem

No examination of the role of the support teacher is possible without considering the relationships between all the participants in the learning situation, that is, support teacher, subject teacher, pupils and parents. For many of the subject teachers having a second qualified and experienced teacher in the lesson is still a fairly new experience, which threatens their previous sovereignty. As one headteacher remarked during the course of my research project, when discussing the change from withdrawing children for remedial work to having teachers supporting in the classroom:

> It was a big change for many teachers to have another teacher in their area – their private empire – and they had to get used to it.

Sometimes it is also a new experience for the support teacher. As more children have been integrated into the mainstream and teaching teams from special schools have been redeployed, a number of these experienced teachers have found themselves supporting their previous clientele in mainstream classrooms. Support teachers are often teachers who have retired early from demanding and responsible positions or who are taking a break from full-time teaching to have more time to contribute to the bringing up of their own families. I have not heard of any teacher, of any age, leaving college with the express ambition of being a support teacher. For pupils and their parents the situation may also be a new one in which relationships now have to be established with both the host and support teachers. It is therefore important that we examine the exigencies of these inter-relationships, focusing in particular on the self-esteem of the various participants.

The Self-esteem of the Support Teacher

The self-esteem of the support teacher is likely to take a daily battering, as described by this woman who had previously held a promoted post in a big primary school:

I have been at my school two years now, but just this morning, when I was trying to persuade a boy to do something, he said to me, 'I don't have to do what you tell me. You're only a helper anyway.' Look, I don't want to go about blowing my own trumpet and saying, 'Look, I'm actually a very capable and qualified teacher,' but I think we have got to do something about raising our status in the eyes of the children, and often in the eyes of our colleagues.

In a society where our perceived status depends very much on what we are paid for doing rather than on our personal qualities, the self-esteem of support teachers can be very dependent on the role they feel they are playing in the classroom. It is always good to hear of subject teachers who do recognise the skills of the support teacher with whom they work and are ready to allow them to play a more satisfying role in the classroom. This kind of co-operation, of course, depends on the tact and the generosity of both teachers. Problems are most likely to arise where one, or both teachers, thinks that the only effective setting for learning is one where the children are silent and the teacher directs everything from the front of the room. I have come across a support teacher who prides herself on taking over classes and showing the subject teacher how it was done when she was in charge. She is in the fortunate position of being able to move off to support another class just as she has undermined her host's confidence and left a class of pupils confused!

It is important that support teachers have an opportunity to meet together regularly and support each other. It is often in these sessions that they are able to value the work they have been doing. In one of the schools where I worked, I often coincided with a very self-effacing elderly man who I later learned was a retired headmaster. He was to be found quietly sitting beside some of the most disruptive pupils in the school, quietly encouraging them and sustaining them to finish tasks that earlier they had not had the confidence to attempt. Later, maybe because of his effectiveness in helping them to catch up with their peers, the funding for his pupils was discontinued and the SENCO organised a little ceremony for his pupils to say goodbye and thank you. At an INSET session, he shared with us his feelings about the tributes paid to him by these pupils:

I found it overwhelming because of what they said. 'Well, I said, is that me? Is that what I've been doing?'

In common with many workers, support teachers are often only fully appreciated when they go. When support teachers meet together and share their concerns and anecdotes, they identify strongly with each other. Perhaps the best way to boost their self-esteem is to realise that if the time comes when they are no longer needed it probably means that they have been successful in helping those children to develop learning habits that enable them to be more independent, or they have given the class-teachers enough confidence to feel that they can now cope with all the needs of the children in their classes.

The Self-esteem of the Subject Teacher

Just as the support teacher is very dependent on the subject teacher for her own self-esteem, so she can do much to build the self-esteem of the subject teacher, or at least guard against diminishing the subject teacher's self-esteem.

There has rarely been a time when teachers have been so pilloried in the press for failing the children they teach. Yet the majority of teachers care intensely about their pupils and work hard to do their job as effectively as possible. Nevertheless it is easy for those outside the profession to point out that teachers rarely work for more than six weeks without a break, and finish their 'real work' before four o'clock. I cannot think of any other job where an employee has to face up to five different groups of thirty critical adolescents each day, and, week after week, hold their attention, energise them into producing work, enable them to work together in a constructive way, and constantly offer encouragement to those least likely to bring her credit. The teacher also has to make sure that there is enough order in the room to allow everyone to learn, even though some might have no desire to co-operate, and none has actually chosen to be there. In most jobs, if employees feel a little below par they can re-organise their work to pace the day a little; but the good teacher has to show enthusiasm to deal with whatever is on the timetable for that slot, and has to show as much animation last period on a Friday as any other time in the week.

Any one who has lived with adolescents will realise how critical they are of their teachers. Often, in trying to create their own identity, they are not just concerned with teaching style, effectiveness and discipline but also how their teachers look and dress, how they talk and their mannerisms and personality weaknesses. The responsibility of being a role model for many young people can put tremendous strain on any teacher, especially one who is only just gaining confidence in his or her new role. A half-overheard remark of a child, or indeed a colleague, can undermine the confidence of a teacher.

In these circumstances, is it surprising that subject teachers sometimes feel vulnerable when a second teacher is in the room, almost as an observer since he or she does not have the strain of preparing the lesson, does not have to settle the class down, and might not even have to do any marking?

It is very tempting for a support teacher to want to show the subject teacher that she is also a competent teacher with qualifications and experience. Much of the literature about support in the classroom talks about an interchangeable partnership, with the support teacher often taking the lesson while the subject teacher temporarily takes the subsidiary role. My own view however is that because secondary school subject teachers are specialists it is totally valid that they should take the lead in the lesson unless the support teacher is also a specialist in the same area. Nevertheless the non-specialist support teacher can have an invaluable role in the secondary school classroom, as discussed in the previous chapter. She can help the subject teacher to understand how the children learn by asking careful questions about the subject being taught. Indeed the non-specialist teacher may have the advantage of appreciating more easily the pupils' problems in understanding technical terms or unfamiliar words and phrases.

How, then, can the support teacher play a significant role in the classroom without threatening the subject teacher's self-esteem? To begin with, the way in which questions are posed by the support teacher to the specialist teacher is very important. It is only too easy to ask a question about the work that conveys the message that the subject teacher's explanation was poor to begin with. Young people, in pure self-defence, often ask questions in this manner, but it would be inexcusable for the support teacher to do this. Often on the occasions when I understand what the teacher has explained, if I see that there are children who did not, I try to be the one who needs a clearer explanation. I am usually apologetic and put it down to the fact that I was preoccupied when the first explanation was given. I often repeat back what the teacher has said in simpler wording as if to confirm that I have understood, but hoping that my protégées benefit from this rephrasing. I am careful to acknowledge the time and trouble that the teacher has taken to answer my question.

If the support teacher can work in this way, it not only saves the subject teacher having to explain again to half a dozen irritable children who blame him or her for their difficulties, but it also shows the pupils that it is alright to have to ask questions; and that if you ask politely and say 'thank you' afterwards the teacher is more likely to smile and act positively towards you. For if pupils learn the skills of seeking help in a constructive manner, this not only helps the pupils asking but also boosts the self-esteem of the teacher sharing her knowledge.

Another issue relates to the problem of giving support in lessons that are poorly taught. However often books, articles in journals and other professionals remind us that it is not the job of a support teacher to judge what goes on in the classroom, we would be inhuman if we did not do so. However it is important that we do not share this judgement with others unless we feel that we are witnessing teaching that could corrupt or be harmful to children in the class. Support teachers do sometimes find themselves in a situation where, week after week, they are sitting through a lesson which falls apart to such an extent that there is little they can support. In such circumstances, there are two possible courses of action. One is to explain to your line-manager that you do not feel your time is best spent in that lesson and leave the line-manager to confirm that with the teacher. Some teachers in whose classes I have supported have welcomed this release from the pressure of having a second teacher to witness their difficulties. However, the second course of action, which has been successful in a number of classes, has been to stay behind after for a few minutes and talk about some part of the lesson which has gone well, or some action of the teacher which has made a real difference to a pupil. When present in such a lesson it is often possible to focus on tremendous strengths and care in some aspects of the interaction between the teacher and the class, despite other shortcomings. Often the teacher is surprised that you have noticed these skills as he or she may well be so worried about the rest of the lesson. If the specialist is ready to acknowledge this, it is possible to discuss ways in which some of the class management could be split between the two of you to give the teacher more time to undertake the individual work he or she is best at.

In one class I supported, this is exactly what happened. The teacher was excellent at encouraging the weaker members of the class, but often lost the rest while he was doing this. For six weeks we agreed that, once he had started the class and explained what had to be done, I would manage the rest of the class and keep everyone on task so that he would have the opportunity to give quality time to individuals without worrying about the rest. In order to reach this stage I had to admit that I had had classes that had been a problem to me, and I suggested we experimented with this situation. By introducing ideas for the class with 'I wonder if...', he felt that he was making the decisions, and I made sure that he told me what role he wanted me to play, even if I had sown the seeds of the idea. Because he then did not have to have to endure constant negative interactions with some of the more disruptive pupils, he was able to give them some of his valued individual attention. Gradually, with his permission, I started bringing in differentiated work cards so that those who finished quickly had a new challenge. This often involved finding information in reference books and the computer instead of engaging in idle chatter. The pupils earned appropriate credits and the noise level dropped sharply.

It was important throughout, however, that the teacher was seen to be in charge and that my input was very much on a 'helper' level. At the end of the half term I had to move on, but this young man was eager to report back to me his success with this class. He has shown me an excellent set of carefully differentiated work cards he made for the next topic and said how much some of the pupils have improved in their attitude to work. Had I instead waded in and tried to discipline the class and extend the brighter ones without his permission, I would have destroyed what little self-esteem he had at that point instead of building it.

Of course, it is not always possible to work in this way and it requires generosity and trust from the subject teacher as well as tact from the support teacher. The general tactics, however, are clear enough. It is important for subject teachers' self-esteem that there is opportunity for them to:

- share their concern about difficult pupils in a non-threatening situation;
- share strategies that work with individual pupils;
- co-operate in planning for individual children;
- meet together regularly to evaluate the effectiveness of their planning;
- achieve all this in a tightly manageable time-schedule.

Well organised joint problem solving meetings are useful in this context. These are described fully in Hanko (1985) *Supporting Special Needs in Ordinary Classrooms*. Although I am now going to give a brief description of how such a meeting works, I do feel that Hanko's book is necessary reading before implementing these groups.

Before a joint problem solving meeting is held, it is important to arrange a suitable time and to agree the length of meeting with all those who teach the pupil or pupils to be discussed. Since each meeting needs a commitment of teacher time it is important that the time required is known by all participants and the meeting begins and ends on time.

A meeting is best divided into three parts, with each part requiring about the same input of time. During the first part, everyone has the opportunity to give some information on the child. It must be established from the start that this is a confidential professional meeting, so that hearsay (for example, about events at the child's home or at the youth club) might be contributed only as long as the source can be acknowledged, and, during the time allowed, any knowledge, however old, can be given. It is important during the first part of the meeting, that teachers feel they can report on how they find the child in their class in a totally non-threatening setting. It is therefore probably better for members of the senior management team only to be present if they actually have day-to-day dealings with the child.

During the second part of the meeting, but not before the preliminary information about the child has been shared, everyone is invited to contribute details of any strategy which is effective on every occasion, or it might be the reporting of a device that engaged the child's interest in one or two lessons, or even just where the child uncharacteristically smiled at the teacher or co-operated with another child in the class. During this part of the meeting it is important to obtain as much positive feedback as possible about the child's reaction to the strategies tried. The teacher who has no trouble with him or her must try to remember what precisely it is that really engages this pupil's motivation, for it is that information which will be important to share with colleagues. The child's out of school pursuits and hobbies are relevant in this section or in the first section.

It is important that neither of these sections overrun the time allocated, however much people want to say, as it is in the last section that a united plan of action is made. Everyone, with as much knowledge as possible of the child and of what has worked, will decide on realistic aims and agree on a way ahead. A scribe will be needed to record this plan, which will need to be read aloud, agreed and distributed to all members of the meeting as soon as possible. Before the time is up the date and time of a follow-up meeting must be agreed. It is often a good idea to have someone responsible for watching the clock so that there is no risk of running out of time before each section has achieved its aim.

I have found these meetings successful and fairly popular with

teachers. I think that by strictly regulating their length, one acknow-
ledges the value of teachers' time. It is probably better to allow an
hour per child initially, but the task can be done in 45 minutes once
teachers are used to this way of working. The strict time limit means
that the participants tend to be concise and prioritise what they say,
often making sure that what is relevant to the meeting has been
decided beforehand. A copy of the plan for the next few weeks can
be given to the appropriate member of the senior management team.

It is important that support teachers acknowledge the good practice that they see in the classroom. I believe that few teachers are
truly so confident in their practice that the endorsement of a
colleague does not build their self-esteem. I support a thirteen-year-
old boy with whom I have great difficulty, even in a one-to-one situation. He is the dread of most of his teachers, even those with years
of experience, so I was worried when I found that a newly qualified
teacher was going to teach him for two of his subjects, a total of
seven periods a week. However, I have since been delighted to
suggest that others ask this teacher for advice on how she manages
to engage him so well in her subjects, English and R.E. She has had
no more trouble with him than with any other child in her well-
ordered classes. Her self-esteem must have gained from her
acknowledged success with this boy, and there is no doubt that she
has increased his self-esteem by giving him work in which he could
succeed, recognising, for instance, that he is better at speaking than
writing (she will accept homework on tape) and ensuring that all her
interactions with him, and the rest of her pupils, are positive rather
than negative. In my experience some of the teachers who have
recently qualified seem to have an encouraging awareness of the
importance of self-esteem in the classroom.

The Self-esteem of the Pupil

Developing a pupil's self-esteem is possibly the most important
single role of the support teacher. When listening to support teachers
talking about their role as described in the last chapter, the one
generally successful aspect of the job they were able to define was
their role in building the child's self-esteem. It is rarely acknowledged how many children in our schools suffer a form of depression
that is linked inextricably with a failure to have confidence in their
own value as a human being. Many of the children who give us most
cause for anger and concern fall into this category. As an adult it is
difficult to remember what it was like to be a child and to have so

little control over one's own life. This situation is even worse for children who are receiving mixed messages from the adults around them.

At any one time ten children in a class of thirty will be living in families which no longer contain both of their birth parents. Of these, four might well still be going through the effect of radical reorganisation, or disorganisation, of their lives at home. In a secondary school this might be the second time it has happened in the child's life. For many children school provides the only stability and certainty in their lives, and is certainly the safest place to off-load some of the anger and despair they feel. *How to Cope with Childhood Stress: A Practical Guide for Teachers,* edited by Pippa Alsop and Trisha McCaffrey (1993), is a useful book to give teachers insight into the lives of many of the children they teach.

Sadly, we can rarely change the lives of the children once they leave school at the end of each day. However, support teachers are in an unrivalled position to help children understand some of the consequences of handling their depression inappropriately and causing more trouble for themselves at school. Many of the children we are asked to support, especially those with behavioural difficulties, will benefit from being helped to examine carefully the negative interactions they have with teachers. Support teachers must be prepared to accept that once the child gains confidence in them they might start to share some of their problems with them. How this is handled will depend on the pastoral organisation of the school, but it will be important to show the child that you are interested and concerned about him or her as a person. Remember, there is often little anyone could, or indeed should, do to change a child's home life, but a child can feel good in knowing another adult who is ready to recognise his or her problems and feelings and to acknowledge the maturity he or she is showing in handling the situation.

One of the advantages of being a support teacher is that the onus is not on you to settle the children at the start of the next lesson. If a stressed child talks to a subject teacher, however caring, the teacher usually has to rush on to the next class, but the support teacher often has some flexibility in this respect. An apology to the teacher of the next class is usually accepted as subject teachers are usually well aware of the needs of their pupils which they do not have time to address.

Children who live in chaotic and stressful homes are often put under additional stress at school because of missing items of school uniform, P.E. gear and other equipment, since such things have low priority in home situations where the adults are still needing support. Support teachers are in an ideal position to check with their protégées at the beginning of the day that they have these things. Sometimes they can lend spare items of equipment, or at least act as an advocate in smoothing the child's path with the staff who might later be reprimanding them about the missing items. Even the hardest hearted Head of year will often lend the spare school tie or P.E. gear to a struggling child. The children who realise that they are worthy of this kind of special help from other adults not only have good role models but receive a boost to their self-esteem.

The support teacher also can often speak to children who are in constant trouble for not doing their homework. There are many reasons for children being unable to do homework in their own homes. It may be that such pupils, with the help of the support teacher, can be encouraged to negotiate with their teachers a time and place to complete this within school or they might be able to direct the child to one of the library homework centres run by some LEAs.

I was intrigued by two pupils who seemed quite content to be in detention every evening. Unknown to them, concern was expressed about their constant inclusion in the detention list and their teachers were asked to try to avoid putting them in detention for a few days. However, although the teachers duly turned a blind eye to some of their peccadilloes, the pair still turned up for detention and pleaded to be allowed in, even to have it 'credited' to them for a later date! When asked why they wanted to be there, they said it was good because the teacher talked to you and helped you do your work, and sometimes you could get your homework done. These two streetwise thirteen-year-olds had tremendous need for individual attention even if they could only obtain it in a negative mode.

Not all children who display inappropriate behaviour in class do so because of the stresses of their home lives. For many it is the stresses of their school lives that cause them to fight back with disruptive or disaffected behaviour. The self-esteem of a child with a book or folder full of uncompleted, shoddy work is often at rock bottom. Some children with moderate or specific learning difficulties have to suffer so many doubts and misgivings when they start a piece of work that, unless they are helped to overcome them, they will waste time and be disruptive. They will either spend ages writing, erasing and rewriting the date and the heading, or they will complete this stage and then avoid further commitment by finding, or creating, such distractions as a broken pencil, a leaking pen, a need to go to the lavatory or an engrossing conversation with a neighbour. The presence of a support teacher for these children is an absolute necessity if the specialist teacher is to be able to engage the attention of the whole class. The first piece of completed work in an exercise book will be a tremendous boost to the child's self-esteem. For that reason I think it is valid to provide more help than you would aim to do on subsequent occasions. At the same time it is easy to develop the habit of 'over-helping' rather than patiently triggering the pupil to gradually take over more of the work. At secondary stage pupils are quite clear about what is actually their work and what the teacher has done on their behalf. The feeling of being patronised will destroy any self-esteem that has been built.

The next two chapters will deal with the different needs of those with moderate learning difficulties and those with specific reading difficulties. However it is relevant to point out at this stage that it is not always appropriate to expect the same work from each child in the class. The concept of differentiation in the classroom has always been with us but in recent years has been much more widely discussed and written about (see the final chapter for some thoughts about this). Some secondary schools have written into their policy that differentiation will be by output, i.e. the same work will be given but each child will do it to their own level. For this strategy to be successful the work must be very carefully planned to be open-ended and not necessarily insisting on a written response. The chances are that some teachers will set pieces of work that will be marked on set criteria, especially in these days of increased rigidity of attainment targets etc., and it will be clear to the weaker children that they cannot succeed in the aims of the work. It is not sufficient for the teacher to tell them to draw a picture as an afterthought, or give them praise for their efforts at work they can see is not as good as others. A support teacher will have to use great tact to find out the content and aims of the lesson beforehand, so that she can offer to bring along tasks which will build up the self-esteem of the child with learning difficulties, instead of making that child feel a failure yet again.

Fortunately the 'slimmed down' revised National Curriculum Orders to be implemented in September 1995 have useful recommendations to aid access to every subject of the curriculum for children with special educational needs. In allowing a judicious amount of flexibility it should be possible to plan work which will lead to success for most children in mainstream classes. These recommendations are the result of consultation with teachers of children with special needs.

An important factor in building up a secondary school pupil's self-esteem is in the body language we use when talking to him or her. I believe that with secondary school pupils you speak as adult to adult. If it is obvious that the young person does not understand words I am using, I repeat the statement again using more familiar vocabulary, but I would never speak to a young person in a different tone or with less courtesy that I would speak to another adult. Some books stress the importance of adults in charge of pupils assuming a physical presence that is dominant (Beynon 1985, Robertson 1981). For support teachers, however, there is a danger that this practice could hinder much of the special work that they are able to contribute to building up the self-esteem of pupils. There are advantages in being in a position where you are not expected to establish dominance in order to control large numbers of unruly youngsters, even if it sometimes bruises one's own self-esteem.

Self-esteem and Parents

The Government's Parents' Charter and the DfE Code of Practice say many fine words about the importance of parents as partners in their children's education. For many parents, however, these words will remain mere rhetoric unless they can feel more comfortable when visiting the school. The incidents of parents behaving aggressively when visiting school is often similar to that of their children who behave aggressively in class until they begin to feel valued for themselves and for the work they do.

There has been a welcome change in policy by some schools which put as much stress on writing and telling parents when things are going well in school as they do when everything is going wrong and their offspring is about to be excluded. However it is still more likely that most of the interactions that many parents have with schools are negative ones. These same parents may well still carry feelings of failure about their own schooling as many parents of children with learning and behavioural difficulties had similar problems themselves (Mason 1992). It is hardly surprising that some parents are so reluctant to put themselves in a position to have their fragile confidence undermined that they cannot even face coming to their child's statement review.

If the school agrees, some of a support teacher's time may be well spent establishing a working relationship with the parents of the child being supported. The support teacher is in such a close relationship with the child that the parents might well find it easier to talk to him or her rather than to the specialist teachers or the year Head. I find it easiest, on the first visit, to give children I am supporting a lift home from school and let them introduce their parents to me. We are such important advocates for the children we support that it is important to give them the option of being in on this first meeting with their parents. Once the parents realise that you are on the side of their child it is usually easy to establish a rapport with them. They are also often happier about attending statement reviews if they know the support teacher will be there, and on the first occasion they might find it reassuring to be accompanied in the waiting room and to be seated near the support teacher during the meeting. If it is obvious that other professionals are speaking in jargon that excludes the parents, it is easier for the support teacher to request a 'translation'. If the parents views are being ignored or glossed over, it is important to draw attention to this fact.

For almost all parents, it is an ordeal to sit in a formal meeting to discuss the problems of their child. Their enforced presence there can only be justified if they are going to be listened to and their opinions valued and acknowledged. It is therefore important that they leave feeling that they had a full share in any decision made about their child's future. The meeting might have been a very humdrum, everyday event for most of the participants, but for the parents it might have been a major threat to their fragile self-esteem, especially if they have, as children themselves, or on behalf of other offspring, been involved in any social services case conferences.

Recently a new element has crept into the relationship between schools and some parents. As schools have been encouraged to compete for pupils and league tables of results have been published, senior management teams have felt a new vulnerability. This vulnerability could effect the relationship of schools with parents, especially the parents of children with special needs. As the new Code of Practice puts a greater onus on schools to provide for the special needs of more and more of their pupils, some children might even find themselves in the position of knowing that no local school is willing to offer them a place at primary/secondary school transfer. At any rate some schools might find that, because of their weak position in the league tables, if they want to stay 'in business' they have to accept the children that no other school will take. In any system that is set up to create winners there are, unfortunately, bound to be losers.

In an educational system that is in danger of damaging the self-esteem of many teachers at all levels when their school is declared to be a 'failing' school in the inspectors' report, and which damages the self-esteem of whole families when this is the only school that will accept their children, it is to be hoped that there are still sensitive support teachers to make the children and their parents feel valued. Self-esteem is the quality that makes people able to take on new challenges and gives them the confidence to make plans and have dreams. It is difficult to see how this decade will be remembered as a time of educational progress if sections of the population are robbed of this investment in the future.

CHAPTER 3
Supporting Pupils with Mild and Moderate Learning Difficulties

Before the 1981 Education Act the children who are the subject of this chapter would have spent their entire school-days, in many LEAs, in the segregated setting of a special school. These schools catered for children who were referred to as ESN (educationally subnormal); but the nomenclature of the eighties, in an effort to move away from the medical deficit model, renamed them schools for children with MLD (mild or moderate learning difficulties). Nowadays it is no longer a foregone conclusion that the pupils in these schools will spend their complete school career there. Unlike in the days before the 1981 Act, the statements of pupils with special needs must be reviewed every year and an assessment made of their current needs – which can, in some cases, involve transfer to a mainstream school.

In the secondary school, support teachers will largely be dealing with those children who have unsuccessfully struggled all their lives to keep up with their classmates but have never drawn attention to themselves so much that their teachers have insisted on their removal to a segregated setting. Since the 1981 Education Act, there has been marked reluctance to send any child to a special school unless they are adversely affecting the education of the other children in the class. However, there are a few children in secondary schools who have spent much of their earlier school life in a special school and are in the process of being reintegrated into mainstream. Some of these children have already had some experience of mainstream in primary school, and have therefore had to cope with two complete changes of school, and others will have been transferred at the primary/secondary school transfer. The first group will have low expectations of their ability to succeed and might have already developed all kinds of strategies to divert attention from themselves and their work. The latter group might well have experienced exceptional success in a segregated, sympathetic setting. They are often eager to join in with the class as they will have been used to having attention from the teacher. Both groups will need a great deal of support and attention to the differentiation of their work.

The aims of integration

Even now, a decade and a half since the deliberations recorded in the Warnock Report (DES 1978) and over a decade since the 1981 Education Act has been implemented, it is useful to reflect on the aims of integration since this has implications for support strategies. Few teachers who have qualified in the last decade would be comfortable with the concept of pupils being denied all contact with their 'normal' peers because they had a difficulty in aspects of their physical, sensory or cognitive development. The move to integrate pupils into mainstream classes and to provide individually planned compensation for their needs in that context was rightly seen as a step, if not a giant stride, in the right direction. The logical accompaniment to this was the move to make it more difficult to segregate children to start with. The former Special Education (SE) forms, which were filled in when teachers felt a child would be better catered for in a segregated school, were replaced by what became known as the 'Warnock stages' (after the landmark Warnock Report of 1978), where a process was begun to formulate what extra intervention was required to enable that child to have equal access to the curriculum in the mainstream. Sixteen years after the publication of the Warnock Report came the Code of Practice from the DfE (1994) which defines the stages in the identification and assessment of special needs very clearly. There will be a more detailed account of the Code of Practice in the final chapter.

The aim in 1981, as it is today, was to make the curriculum of the school accessible to all children. There was realisation that some aspects of the curriculum would need to be modified for children with special needs if they were to be allowed to learn at a suitable pace for themselves, and if they were to feel successful. The concept of 'differentiation' of teaching materials became all-important as teachers realised that mixed ability teaching was expanding its boundaries at both ends, but particularly at the lower end.

The aim was that difficulties in learning should not isolate a child from neighbourhood friendship groups and the opportunity to participate in the full range of the curriculum, social and sporting activities offered by a school. During the early and mid-eighties, the practical aim in secondary schools was often to reintegrate those children who had been in segregated provision during their primary school years. These were children who had often had considerable success in their segregated setting and were believed to be able to cope with the social side of mainstream life. The first children to be reintegrated were often the children of parents who had been vociferous in wanting this for their children and were therefore very supportive of both the child and the school.

Unfortunately the aim of a few LEAs was to close their special schools in order to divert the money to be used elsewhere. Although this could well have been an appropriate long-term result of integration which was carefully planned for the good of the children in these schools, it caused problems in being pushed ahead too quickly. Children were earmarked for integration before their teachers considered they were ready and before their parents had accepted the advantages of the move. This meant much goodwill was lost in the early stages as schools were persuaded to accept larger numbers of pupils who needed a great deal of support, and whose parents were concerned about the suitability of the placement for their child.

There were, however, considerable successes in integration where there was co-operation between the special school, mainstream school, the parents and the professionals. Good integration is unlikely to follow an initiative which is basically a cost-cutting exercise since integration of slow learning children is very dependent on extra professional support in the classroom and the staff room.

No one can overestimate the importance of not only planning ahead for integration, but also adhering to the plan for systematic support, even if it means delaying the date for total integration. An example of failure to honour this principle occurred at a recent statement review which I attended, where it was decided, with regret, to place a thirteen-year-old girl back in the special school from which she had been integrated into a mainstream school ten months before. She was unhappy and socially isolated because the plan for her integration had not been followed through. The arrangements initially envisaged two terms of part-time attendance at the mainstream school, initially totally supported by a teacher from her special school, but this support was to diminish in the second term, when she would receive support from one of the mainstream school's own support teachers. In the event the teacher from her special school left for promotion so the arrangements planned for the first two terms were left out, and Helen was transferred during the third term when the school's own support teachers were already fully committed. A peripatetic teacher, who had not worked in this school before, was allocated to support Helen for four afternoons a week, but because of her other commitments she was never there when Helen needed reassurance at break-times and lunch-times. She was also as lost as Helen was when she came into the school, reinforcing Helen's feeling of helplessness. When she went on prolonged sick-leave during Helen's second and third term at the school, the situation was past retrieval. Clearly situations like this must be avoided through careful planning and appropriate support, and it is to this issue we now turn.

Successful integration

How would we define successful integration? If one of the aims of integration is to increase social opportunities, we must look at the child and see if he or she is part of the kind of friendship group that most children enjoy. If the child is isolated in the playground, or the butt of jokes and always the fall guy in playground games, perhaps support in the playground is needed for integration to be successful. If the child is unable to join in any lessons without adult support, that situation has to be looked at closely in case it is making the child over-dependent rather than encouraging independence. While the employment of support teachers depends on the revenue from individual statements, there is sometimes a fear on the part of the support teacher that she will outlive her usefulness. However, a child who is unable to move into any kind of independence in a mixed-ability classroom (for example, in drama, food technology, art and the oral part of humanities lessons) may not be ready for integration. Contrasting illustrations from my own work will help to illustrate the point.

The first example is of Kevin, a fourteen-year-old boy who attended the local special school from the age of nine until the age of thirteen. He has elderly foster parents who have looked after him since he was a toddler and who are very supportive of whatever professionals feel is best for Kevin. They have attended all meetings about him, and were very swift to respond to the school when Kevin truanted on two occasions with another boy in his class. Now at a mainstream secondary school, Kevin still has a great deal of difficulty with his work but will not tolerate the direct intervention of a support teacher. When I am supposed to be supporting him, I therefore locate another boy with similar difficulties, move him within earshot of Kevin and teach this other boy in a voice that I know will carry to Kevin. Kevin is then in a position to chose whether he accepts the help or carries on in his own way. He often submits work that is unfinished and which is inferior to some of the neat but largely less demanding work which he did at his special school. He sits with a group of the class reprobates and joins in passing notes and *risqué* pictures with them during some lessons. He has on a couple of occasions truanted with one of them and he often finds himself in detention at the end of the day, though he has also managed to get himself into the house football team and is a reserve for the Under 15 second XI. His foster parents are disappointed that he does not join any school clubs.

The second example concerns Hayley who is twelve years old. She went to the same special school as Kevin from the age of eight until she was eleven, but was transferred to her original primary school just one term before secondary school transfer. The staff of this school were not happy about her reintegration as no funds were available to give her the support they felt she needed. There was also a dispute between her parents: her mother wanted her to transfer to a very large secondary school, whereas the professionals recommended a smaller secondary school. Her father agreed to the professionals' judgement. Although mother refused to visit the second school, a place was offered and accepted by Hayley's father and Hayley started there in September. Hayley reads well, better than many in her class, but with little understanding. She writes very neatly but her work is repetitious and uncreative. She knows most of her multiplication tables and can add and take away as competently as many in her class. With an IQ of 92 she would be seen as an essential case for reintegration.

Unfortunately, Hayley spends most of her time wandering around on her own. She is frequently in tears and makes a bee-line for any adult who approaches. In a P.E. lesson she stands helplessly after an activity, waiting for her group to reclaim her. When I am supporting her she frequently complains of being tired, and if I try to make her persevere with a task she either demands to be allowed to go to the lavatory or simply bursts into tears and yet she is eager for me to sit next to her, and if I briefly help a neighbouring child she will take my hand or touch my face to bring me back to her.

Although Hayley has a higher IQ than Kevin and has been reintegrated at an earlier stage, the integration has not in any way fulfilled its aims. In fact, we fear it might be necessary to return the child to the segregated setting where she had friends, of whom she still speaks and writes in her stories. She is patently unhappy and is beginning to refuse to go to school, and the parents' conflicts over her education make it difficult for them to support her in school.

What are we to make of these two cases? I see Kevin's reintegration as successful, despite the fact that he is often in trouble at school. His IQ is well below Hayley's, but his social skills within the group he operates are more than adequate. He has also managed to relate with his chosen group within the school setting without threatening his relationship with his foster parents as he still keeps their rules, and he accepted their punishment with equanimity when they grounded him for a few days for his truancy. In contrast, Hayley's integration is manifestly unsuccessful because it is purely locational since she can only cope when she has one-to-one support.

In secondary schools we have some children who 'pre-Warnock' would have received segregated education from an early stage of their primary schooling. However they have remained in mainstream throughout. Most of the time they have caused concern to their teachers because of their inability to match the progress of the rest of the class, and the gap between their performance and that of their peers has become more obvious by the time they have reached secondary school. Peter and his twin Paul were two such children. Both were born prematurely into a large, loving family. They both had low birth weights and Peter was four weeks old, and Paul six weeks old, before they left hospital. They are now fourteen years old and are often in the same lessons. Peter's work is untidy and badly written and he relies greatly on the girl beside whom he is sitting, often copying her work, word for word. In contrast, Paul's work is immaculately tidy and well written but he also relies a great deal upon the girl beside whom he sits. Both the boys are very popular with the girls as they are nice looking and take a great pride in their appearance and personal freshness. Although Peter has more independence in spelling and working out his own calculations teachers tend to perceive Paul as being brighter as his work is always well-presented. There is much good natured rivalry between the boys, and one of the girls remarked to me that, 'although Paul is cuter, Peter is more of a laugh'. They both look forward to leaving school and joining the family building firm. The staff at the school are split between demanding that they be moved to a more suitable (i.e. a special) school before Year 10 and acknowledging that they are just as well where they are. They are entirely honest about their need to copy the work of other pupils, and acknowledge that they chose their helpers well. This dependence on their classmates in no way diminishes their social standing among their own group of friends.

Jason is also fourteen. He is the younger of two brothers, both of whom have needed in-class support. He is an undersized boy and has very dry fair hair which refuses to lie flat against his head. He is called 'Peanut' by most of his year group, and indeed many other children in the playground. When I asked him if he enjoyed having a nickname he was quite definite that he did not like to be called by this name. Despite the fact that a deputy head has asked staff to reprimand pupils who call Jason by this nickname, I have heard teachers calling him this, even in class.

The first time I saw Jason I went into a classroom without having met him before. I quickly identified him as he was obviously not able to join in the lesson in any way. When the teacher was writing on the board, other children removed his rubber and ruler and forced him to beg for their return. As he left the classroom a boy who claimed to be his friend let his bag swing in his face. On the way to the next lesson I walked with the two boys, and the 'friend' explained to me his role in looking after 'Peanut'. In the next lesson (R.E.) Jason was the only child who did not at any time join in an animated discussion on Easter customs, despite the teacher's sensitive attempts to ask him about hot cross buns and Easter eggs. During the weeks I supported Jason, it was only when I withdrew him that I was able to make any headway with him. His progress was slow, but he was happy with withdrawal and his parents requested that it should happen more often. After discussion with other professionals and with the parents, it was agreed that Jason was not benefiting from remaining in the mainstream and he would profit from the bridging course that the local special school ran to ease the passage of pupils from school to FE College. Jason transferred to special school the Easter before Year 10, and has managed to make friends with two boys and a girl in his class. They no longer use school transport, but go to and fro by bus, and they sometimes can be seen sitting on a seat, apparently deep in conversation, in one of the shopping parades where they change buses.

The above two examples demonstrate another set of contrasting experiences. Again, the aims of integration had been satisfied in one case but not the other, although it is possible that Peter and Paul would have benefited from a different teaching approach at special school.

In order for integration to work, the traditional attitudes and expectations of teachers have to change as much as those of children and their parents. Dessent (1987) warns:

Expertise in special needs is often more to do with knowing what cannot be done than knowing what can be done. Living with educational failure and making appropriate and teaching adjustments to redefine what counts as 'success', is, at the end of the day, what expertise in special needs is about. (p.85)

He goes on to say:

Support services in ordinary schools have rarely addressed the issue of educational failure. They have traditionally operated on a 'success' or 'curative' model...If children with special needs are to be educated appropriately within mainstream education then a major requirement must be that mainstream teachers learn to live with the relative 'failure' of pupils in traditional educational skills. (p.85)

This was written before 'league tables' became a reality!

How can integration fail special pupils?

The Audit Commission (1992) has focused on concerns about how monies intended to implement successful integration have been allowed to drift in schools because of lack of accountability. Much of the drifting of special resources from one child to another is actually done for the best of motives. There are many special needs specialists who are reluctant to risk stigmatising a statemented child by asking a support teacher to work specifically with that child, and so support is put into the classroom on a very general basis for all the pupils' benefit. I have come across support teachers who are regularly working in classrooms, paid by the integration fund money which is attached to a statement of special needs, but they do not know which is the statemented child.

I fully understand the sensitivity of the SENCO who runs the special needs department in this manner. However, I feel that if a child's needs are definable enough to be the subject of a statement, it is unlikely that other children in the class are not aware of the pupils who need help. During the course of my study on support, one boy with severe specific learning difficulties but good insight into his problems said:

Sometimes people are embarrassed about having a support teacher, but often they are embarrassed about not being able to read and having to go up to the teacher and ask all the time...The teacher is there to help me, but there is someone else in the classroom who has absolutely no need whatever, who thinks, there's another teacher in the classroom...I might as well make life easier for myself as well...I don't think it's fair when the person can get on perfectly well without him or her. (Year 9 boy)

Another boy however did have a rather different attitude:

> I know I need the help but I don't want it to be obvious. If a support teacher helps me I like others to think it's because she likes me. (Year 9 boy)

A couple of Year 7 boys whom I questioned about support could not understand why I linked it with embarrassment. They listed things which would embarrass them, in the classroom, but having a support teacher was not among them as they had been supported throughout their primary years.

Unfortunately I was not able to record the opinion of a child with moderate learning difficulties. From my experience, however, I feel that in the early years of secondary school such children have few reservations about being helped by a second adult in the room. Most of the children I support are friendly and welcome the extra attention.

As a support teacher allocated to a specific statemented child, my priority is to look at the recommendations on the statement and concentrate on finding ways to implement these. Often, however, the aims written on the statement are totally different from those of the teacher in whose room you are working; yet the support teacher is there to serve the teacher as well as the child. Perhaps the teacher has decided she wants a specific piece of work completed by all the class by the last lesson before half-term. There you are, in a science lesson, with a child who is able to complete the work because he is able to write neatly and correctly, and is very eager to please, especially the teacher. On the other hand he does not actually understand the processes about which he is about to write. As a teacher you would like to go over it again with him, using different vocabulary and slowing down at some points for him to grasp what is happening; but, if you do this, the piece of work will not be ready to give in at the end of the lesson so you decide to give him a lot of help with the work, you might even have to write it out for him to copy, and you know he will have the satisfaction of giving in a neat, praiseworthy piece of work, like everyone else, at the end of the lesson.

On one level this has been a valid activity as the child has been seen to be at one (i.e. integrated) with the class. He has also been praised for his neat work in front of the class (and only one child remarked that the support teacher had given him a lot of help). Yet on another level he is reaching that point in science lessons when it is less likely that he will be able to grasp the concepts that several of the others are also finding difficult, and very few will use in everyday life. Perhaps the experience of fitting in with this group is as important as learning on a level that he can understand.

If this is so, will it be important for him to be entered for examinations with this class; and, if so, are we going to help him, or are we going to allow him to fail? Even if we were allowed to help him, this would invalidate league tables and mislead employers. However, if we are not going to expect him to succeed in the same examinations, why are we not using the resources to help him to build up skills which he will need later, and which could later be validated externally in the 'Wordpower' and 'Numberpower' schemes? Maybe he can, with extra effort, obtain a GCSE grade in English and Maths with extra teaching and suitable classwork, but the decision might have to be made to withdraw him for some of the time. Perhaps individual educational plans and the post 14+ reviews recommended in the Code of Practice will help to resolve this. (The piloting of vocational courses for 14–16 year olds in some secondary schools after September 1994, and the judicious flexibility written in to the access recommendations in the revised National Curriculum Orders, should provide more motivation for this group of pupils.)

The change to in-class support from teaching special groups of 'remedial' children who proceeded up the school, cocooned with their kindly teacher in 'the hut', is a welcome one as long as we realise that these children still have the need to be taught some subjects or topics at a pace at which they can succeed. Unfortunately, some of the areas of school life where they could excel have now been replaced by other subjects. For example, Food Technology, with its emphasis on experimentation and process, does not give the slow learner the same opportunity for tangible success as its predecessor, Home Economics, where the product was important and a plate of uniformly jammy tarts could be passed round the group.

I very much like the idea of a support workshop described in Bell and Best (1986):

> ...a room has been prepared with individual work carrels and stocked with teaching machines, language consoles, cassette-recorders, reading schemes, problem-solving materials, spelling programmes, numeracy games, sets of comprehension exercises, extension work and so on...to minimise the disruption in the child's classroom work, the workshop session itself runs for no longer than fifteen minutes, the children leaving their normal classroom to discuss their progress and collect the next

instalment of material aimed at developing a specific skill. Obviously these arrangements are not made on an *ad hoc* basis and negotiation has to take place between the class teacher and the support teacher to agree the most suitable and convenient times for children to attend these short sessions. (p.102)

There are a number of advantages in this kind of arrangement. The really clever child in the class might well go along before or after the one with learning difficulties, since extension work as well as remedial work is based in this room. A child whose only problem is his handwriting is as likely to be booked in for a workshop session as the child who needs help in understanding basic concepts. It is also very good use of the support teacher's time and expertise, as she would be constantly engaged in planning for children and interacting with them rather than sometimes sitting listening to a lesson, unable to intervene or plan in any way. On the other hand the child is only being withdrawn for a specific time, and with a specific well-defined aim, and will shortly be returning to mainstream provision.

Making support successful

Making support successful is a very important responsibility of both of the teachers in the room. This is even more so when children know that the support is directed to them and not just generally available in the classroom as the following example illustrates.

Billy flatly refused to accept any support. He would put his arms protectively around his work and refused to let any support teacher see what he was doing. Often he had nothing to hand in at the end of the lesson. The teacher invariably asked any support teacher in the room to help Billy, and seemed frustrated that no one did. On investigating this case, it emerged that Billy had accepted support in lower forms but had still found his work difficult because he had quite severe learning problems. Other children had pointed out that even with support he had not done well. He now seemed to feel – understandably – that it was worse to fail with support than on your own.

Perhaps if there had been more time for the teachers to confer, Billy could have done a different piece of achievable work which would have been both acceptable to the teacher and within his grasp so that he would have had a successful outcome. One of the great difficulties with supporting pupils in secondary schools is the lack of time and opportunity for teachers to confer together about individual pupils and their needs. It is also sometimes difficult for support teachers to devise work in subjects which are not their own. Yet it is important for support teachers to do all they can to secure liaison if the support is to be as effective as it can be (see the discussion in Chapter 2).

It seems obvious to say that the route to successful support is through good differentiation. Unfortunately, experts who glibly talk about differentiation often find it difficult to give practical examples in the secondary school. There is one school whose special needs policy simply states that 'differentiation by outcome is available throughout the school'. This hardly needs stating: of course different children give in the work complete or incomplete, well done or not so well done! The key question, however, is how does the child feel whose work is differentiated by outcome when the fact is that he has not one complete piece of work in his book? Would it not be better to offer differentiated or sequenced activities?

Some of the new textbooks in English and Geography have activities at the end of each chapter which are graded in difficulty so that everyone in the class can complete the first one or two with success, and the more able pupils will complete further exercises with a gradual increase of effort and use of such resources as reference books, atlases and dictionaries. I favour sets of 'home made' work cards which are linked to the specific lesson being taught. If the support teacher has had a chance to confer with the subject teacher so that she knows what the next lesson is about, she can produce these. They should each require one complete task to be done. Some tasks can be drawing or copying and some might be oral. Pupils tend to select and work at their own level. If the class is engaged in working on a variety of activities which are germane to the lesson, the teachers have time to listen and help with the oral work which will offer a good indication of how much of the topic has been understood and internalised.

Another method of providing differentiation is to produce a wall-newspaper of the topic being covered. With this method the brightest pupils can be given more demanding tasks requiring a certain amount of research, whereas the slower learners can be given tasks which consolidate that which they are able to grasp. This could be filling the missing words in a short article written by the teacher, or being part of a small group making up a wordsearch using all the most important terms, making up a simple crossword, copying a map or diagram, asking one of the teachers a list of questions and writing down the replies in the form of an interview. It might be possible to use the computer to produce an edition which can be taken home. Because groups of children will produce items between them everyone should be able to see an item with their name under it.

Both these interventions are dependent on the subject teacher being willing for the support teacher to work as a partner. Where there is little communication between the two teachers, either because of time constraints or differences in philosophy, it can be possible to give effective support. Sometimes the most useful support is to encourage the child to think about what he or she is doing, and why. Very often the kind of conversations that parents and grandparents have with little children transfer well to this situation. This is recognised by those who have studied 'thinking skills', also known as 'meta cognition', which is basically, 'thinking about thinking'.

Thinking about thinking

Reuven Feuerstein is an Israeli psychologist who was concerned by children who seemed to find it difficult to learn by experience. He encountered recently immigrated children who were either haphazard and impulsive in their responses, or were passive and inert when faced with a new challenge. He refused to believe this was a lack of intelligence and instead assumed they had never learnt to structure their thinking. To remediate this, he devised a set of activities, or 'instruments,' which were designed to exercise specific areas of the brain. Hence this method has become known as 'Instrumental Enrichment'.

A very important aspect of this method is that it must be used only by people trained in the method. This is considered vital since an essential part of the process is that the child should be talked through each stage. The first instrument, for example, involves placing joining lines through what seem to be random patterns of dots in order to produce a set group of geometrical figures which overlap differently at each stage. As much emphasis is put on the relating each activity to other subjects in the curriculum as is put on the process of completing the actual instrument. The term which describes relating the processes to the curriculum and to everyday tasks is known as 'bridging'.

Few support teachers will have the time or resources to become trained Instrumental Enrichment tutors, but all can benefit from being conscious of the importance of bridging, whatever the activity. For those who would like more information on this subject there are addresses in Appendix 2.

The key characteristic of 'mediating' learning is to help the child to grasp the teacher's intentions. One of the areas which lends itself well to this intervention is the technology lesson. As the second adult in the room the support teacher can look carefully at materials with the child and ponder on why the specialist teacher is using those materials rather than others, or why this task is being set. However it is possible to do this in other lessons, or even in those moments before and after a lesson when nothing is happening. Support teachers who are asked to take part in school trips have an excellent opportunity to focus an individual child on new stimuli and talk through his perceptions.

The important aim of mediation is that the child should not be the passive recipient of learning or of experiences. 'Now I wonder what Mr Brown wants to see in your exercise book', will develop the child's thinking more than, 'Now did you understand that, Mr Brown wants you to...'. 'What do you think Mr Brown will think when he sees this?' is more likely to establish a habit of self evaluation than, 'Come on, read it through before you give it in'.

All Feuerstein's Instruments have on the front page a picture of a child, who could be of either sex, who is obviously wrestling with a problem, and the words, 'Just a minute. Let me think.' I supported a girl who was of low intelligence but desperate to keep up with the class. She was very impulsive and often started her work before the teacher had finished giving the instruction so that she would not get behind. Consequently her marks were disappointing, and by the time I was called in she was presenting behavioural problems. After six individual sessions with her she was taught to listen to the teacher, assume the pose of the child on the cover of the instrument and say to herself, 'Just a minute. Let me think.' She followed these instructions excellently, and, despite substituting, ''ang on. I got to fink abaht it' for the recognised formula, her work improved noticeably.

Blagg (1988), a psychologist working in Somerset, has devised a scheme of thinking skills which are now used in many English schools. The main aim of this course is to improve the self-esteem and confidence of secondary age children by enhancing their ability to learn. The ways in which the Somerset Thinking Skills Scheme aims to do this is as follows:

- the use of a wide range of discussion/problem solving;
- tasks that are relatively free from previous failure experience;
- the inclusion of open-ended tasks where there are many alternative, justifiable interpretations communicating to the pupils that the teacher is not necessarily looking for one correct answer;

- the provision of interesting visuals to stimulate and extend pupil ideas and provide a learning environment that presents tasks in multiple modes;
- the careful sequencing of pupil activities to enable pupils to reinforce and build on basic skills, resources and strategies;
- the emphasis on small group work, enabling pupils to help one another, comparing, sharing and reflecting on the skills, procedures, and solutions.

There are groups of professionals meeting in many areas to share their interest in the role of thinking skills, or meta-cognition, in education. It certainly has a place in the support of special education in mainstream schools. Certainly a short period of carefully guided work on thinking skills a couple of times a week could enhance the performance of children in a class. However the thinking skills exercises, or instruments, need careful delivery if they are to achieve their full potential and are certainly not to be seen as being an easy option for giving out to children to occupy them during registration. The adult mediation of the experience is essential.

How do we measure success?

It is difficult to define success with those children who will never totally catch up with their peers in a society which sees examination results as the main indicator of success. However it is possible to call to mind such pupils who bear more evidence of their success in their life after school than do many of their brighter peers. I recently met a young man who was the most limited pupil I ever taught in a unit for disruptive pupils. He had become disruptive at his special school when he had ceased to make progress by the age of fourteen. He was a very, very angry adolescent and totally refused to make any effort with his school work. He had a talent for copying pictures very accurately and could often be persuaded to copy something about the picture under it. He liked to know what it said and took trouble to memorise whatever he had written under the picture. But I am afraid that this was as near as we were able to approach reading and writing with Matthew.

However, on a group trip to a local Youth Hostel called Tanners' Hatch, in the Surrey countryside, he became a leader. His special school had been in the country, and he knew all about closing gates, climbing stiles, recognising trees by their leaves and nuts, and he could see which sheep were about to lamb and which already had.

He was a different, delightful boy and we were not surprised when the warden invited him to visit again the following weekend to help with a younger party.

I met Matthew recently. He is now 23 and engaged to a girl he met at Tanners' Hatch. They visit there regularly as they are both active conservationists. He has learnt to read and has enough confidence to stand up and speak at meetings. Above all, he is happy and proud of his life. He describes some of his fellow pupils as losers as they have been in trouble with the law. He obviously sees himself as a winner.

Although not every young person can have this kind of success I am sure many readers will call to mind similar stories. It is important that when we support children with learning difficulties we recognise when they can go no further and we give them an opportunity to succeed where they are. I realise that there is a very narrow path to tread between under-extending such pupils and pushing them so hard that they have to resort to distracting behaviour in order to survive. Materials used must be motivating to the individual. Although we now have a national curriculum where the aim of acquiring knowledge is fast catching up with that of understanding and being able to use the process, there is still the possibility, in achieving many of the attainment targets, to use materials which engage the pupil's motivation.

The main aim of support with low achievers must be to foster their independence, and this will not be done unless they have valid cause to be confident. I welcome the recommendations in the Code of Practice for Special Needs (DfE 1994) to have multi-disciplinary reviews at 14+, where young people are to be encouraged to take part in decision-making about their futures. It is very probable that other professionals will see the low achiever-who has survived in a mainstream school as a success. An even greater indicator of success will be if he also has a group of friends with whom he relates as an equal.

A colleague was feeling considerable trepidation on a parents' evening when she knew that she would have to tell the parents of one girl how little progress had been made with her reading. The parents had not visited the school before so the staff were convinced that they were coming because they were dissatisfied. When the parents arrived they shook the teacher's hand and thanked her warmly. It turned out that their daughter was the first member of the family who had actually learned to read well enough to understand the letters and leaflets that came into the house. The parents were proud and delighted as they were aware of and accepted their own difficulties and those of their children. Not only was the girl successful but so were her parents who, despite their difficulties, were both in employment, kept an orderly home and sent polite, well turned out children into school every day.

It is sad that some people can only feel successful after they leave school. For them their school experience can be a betrayal of their right to self-esteem throughout childhood and adolescence. The support teacher who is at the child's side in the classroom is in a privileged position of being able to detect any small step towards understanding and to reinforce this. This should be pointed out to others so that they too can celebrate the success with the child. As advocates of the children they support they must constantly be alert to ways in which to build their pupils' self-esteem.

CHAPTER 4

Supporting Children with Specific Learning Difficulties

Children with specific learning difficulties are the pupils who are most likely to need support in mainstream classrooms. Although I think it important to look at their needs separately from those of the children in the previous chapter, this does not mean that children with moderate learning difficulties might not also have similar specific difficulties also. Children with specific learning difficulties are often, perhaps usually, referred to as being dyslexic. In the Warnock Report (DES 1978) there is some doubt cast on the existence of a 'dyslexia syndrome', but there is recognition of a group of children whose difficulties in specific areas of the curriculum are greater than their general ability would lead one to expect:

> Although there is no agreed criteria for distinguishing those children with severe and long-term difficulties in reading, writing and spelling from others who may require remedial teaching in these areas, there are nevertheless children whose disabilities are marked but whose general ability is at least average, and for whom distinctive arrangements are necessary. (Warnock Report 1978, p.218, 11.48)

There is a lack of agreement on a term to describe children with these specific difficulties both nationally and internationally. However there is no question about the existence of such children and the concern that they cause to their teachers and their parents.

The British Dyslexia Association

The British Dyslexia Association probably has the highest profile of any organisation supporting the needs of pupils in mainstream schools. The concern of parents, whose children were not learning to read despite adequate intelligence, freedom from physical and emotional defect and conventional instruction, led to the setting up of voluntary dyslexia associations. Eight associations were formed between 1965 and 1972. In 1972 the British Dyslexia Association was formed as a national co-ordinating organisation. Its aims are to promote understanding of the problem of dyslexia and to support research into all aspects of the problem. The membership includes parents, teachers, psychologists and anyone interested in the problem of dyslexia.

The BDA produces an annual handbook which is full of information about services available to dyslexic pupils and their parents in the private sector as well as the public sector. It also contains articles on current developments and individual cases. In addition, they produce publications which describe recent research, educational developments and individual case histories. The address is to be found in Appendix 2.

Definitions and descriptions of specific learning difficulties

There have been innumerable attempts to define the causes of specific learning difficulties. Much work was done on trying to establish an organic reason for these difficulties, especially as they seemed often to run in families. There are a number of theories about the way both hemispheres of the brain are connected and there is no shortage of literature which gives detailed explanations of brain function (Tansley and Panckhurst 1981).

A more recent development concentrates on irregularities in the eyesight of some children with 'dyslexic' type difficulties. An American psychologist, Helen Irlen (1983), discovered that certain children were helped to learn to read, or to speed up their reading, by placing a carefully selected tinted overlay on the printed page. The tests to diagnose whether a tinted overlay will help a reading problem is done by teachers who have received a special training as screeners. The children who benefit most are those who report that they see words jump about, wobble or go wavy when they look at a page of print. They are also pupils who become noticeably fatigued when they have to read for a long time. Irlen described the distortion they experienced as the Scotopic Sensitivity Syndrome (SSS). If, after a period of use, this overlay is seen to assist the child's ability to read print, spectacles with specially designed lens to filter light could be made after consultation with a specialist.

Although there has been much scepticism about the efficacy of coloured filters since Helen Irlen's evidence was anecdotal rather than being the result, or part of, a rigorous research project, there have been a number of both lay and professional supporters who can describe instances where the filters have made a dramatic difference in reading ability. Research has now been undertaken by the Medical Research Council's Applied Psychology Unit in Cambridge and the early results of this research are being used by the Institute of Optometrists in this country. Precision equipment has been developed for testing children who might be helped by coloured lens and this is certainly a development welcomed by many professionals concerned with the reading difficulties of this group of children. Much of the skill in prescribing the overlays and filters is concerned with the different tints which are helpful to individual children. It is also a development which parents welcome. The overlays are relatively cheap but the spectacles are still expensive. The use of an overlay is recommended for at least a month before investing in spectacles.

Class teachers and support teachers may well come across pupils who use tinted filters or lens and who are convinced of their usefulness. There is a theory (Cardinal et al. 1993) that these can be useful as a placebo, making children feel their difficulties are being noted and acted upon. They are therefore, in theory, going to make more effort with their work to show this does work. After all, these children will have been the focus of attention from the specialist who has prescribed the filters, and will have had money spent on them by their parents. Also the fact that the child is using an overlay or spectacles with coloured lens demonstrates that his difficulty has been acknowledged and is in the public arena.

The use of filters is gradually being backed up by research and they are becoming available to any child whom they will benefit. The cost is now between £55 and £250 as filters may now be obtained from a number of optometrists. A colorimeter is used for diagnosis. Perhaps when children with difficulties are regularly reviewed in accordance with the DfE Code of Practice, this kind of provision will be resourced without having to proceed all the way to Stage 4 and the statementing process.

It is useful for support teachers, working closely with individual children, and special needs co-ordinators giving advice to subject teachers, to be aware of all the theories and developments in aiding pupils with specific learning difficulties. However, the fact remains that, in a secondary school, our task is to help the child access the curriculum shared by his peers in the best way possible.

The earlier children's difficulties are identified the less difficulty they are likely to have in secondary school. Unfortunately there are some pupils who are not identified until just prior to secondary school transfer, as it is easy to dismiss a child with these difficulties as lazy and unmotivated. If they have been through primary school, experiencing difficulty in every subject, there will probably be a lack of confidence and motivation. However some children blossom in secondary school. One child who did this was Christopher. I was told by my primary school counterpart that he would never cope in the large secondary school to which he was going. Apparently he sat on his own at junior school so there was always room for someone to sit beside him and support him, and he was the only one who never had any of his work displayed. The other children did not want him in the group doing a project. I was expecting to meet a very depressed boy.

Two days after his arrival at secondary school I asked some of his teachers how he had settled in. They asked why such a bright lad was in the lowest band. None of the first years had yet had to hand in any written work but there had been plenty of opportunity to answer questions in class, and to join in with discussions. Christopher had a good vocabulary and general knowledge and had at long last had a chance to shine at school. He had tended to be a 'wanderer' at junior school, so he had responded well to having to walk quite a long way between each lesson. By the time he had to present some written work he had gained confidence in his abilities and was motivated to ask for help at home and at school. He still has some problems, but he no longer sees himself as one big problem.

It is a problem that some children who have been diagnosed, and labelled dyslexic, at an early age see themselves in a totally negative light. One boy told me sadly that he was dyslexic and unless I was a proper 'dyslexia teacher' (i.e. trained by the British Dyslexia Association) I was wasting my time with him. Another parent asked me not to help her son with reading as I would 'mess up the work of his proper dyslexia teacher'. Both boys saw themselves as total problems who could only be helped by certain people. Neither was able to see that there were many, many things they could do as well, if not better, than other children.

Structured Multi-sensory Literacy Programmes

If the child has a statement to support his need for help because of specific learning difficulties, it will nearly always specify that he should have a structured multi-sensory literacy programme. There are a number of programmes available which have been prepared by professionals who have spent many years of their careers working out the best ways to help these children to learn to read, spell and write. Perhaps the most popular is the Alpha to Omega programme (published privately in 1974, now in its fourth edition, Heinemann) which was devised by Beve Hornsby who founded the Hornsby International Centre, which now trains many teachers on both part-time courses and by distance learning. For information about this Centre refer to Appendix 2.

If parents pay for individual tuition for their child with specific learning difficulties, especially if they employ a tutor recommended by the British Dyslexia Association, their child will almost certainly be taught using these materials and these methods in a very structured way. There are many dyslexia tutors who have not received a full teacher training but are specially trained to teach by this method. Children in primary schools who receive help from learning support teams or the school's support teachers may well benefit from these multi-sensory programmes of work. A number of high schools are offering short sessions before and after school for those children with this type of literacy difficulty. These sessions are often during registration or in the children's and the teachers' own time, and they are therefore dependent on the goodwill of teacher and the motivation of the children. It is not easy to provide this kind of support in the secondary school.

It is unfortunate that some children, like the two boys described at the end of the last section, start secondary school believing that this is the only approach to literacy that will help them. The problem with using a multi-sensory programme is that it is best done individually or in a small group. Unless this is offered, as it is by some dedicated teachers, before school begins it will entail withdrawal. As soon as you begin to withdraw from a secondary school classroom you are risking creating problems rather than solving them.

The multi-sensory approach is to learn by seeing, hearing, touching and moving. A support teacher can often create the conditions to approach a science or French text in this way if she carefully keeps the pupils on task, listening to the teacher, following each word with the finger or a guide. Pupils with specific learning difficulties often need help to establish the habit of paying careful attention to the lesson. It is in this way that a support teacher can often be used quite intensively in the first few weeks at secondary school. Once a child gains confidence and experiences some success he will be more motivated to take control of his own learning. One of the advantages of working with secondary pupils in a multi-sensory way is that you can discuss with them what you are doing and why, and encourage them to think of strategies to help themselves.

Strategies for reading difficulties

Since it is not possible to work in a multi-sensory way with all children with specific learning difficulties, I am going to describe ways in which I have helped children and also seen them helped by other teachers. There are many teachers who do not see themselves as experts in any kind of special education who have devised effective, common-sense methods to help most of the children in their classes to learn. It is important that teachers share with each other any successful strategy they have.

If you know a child has difficulty with reading and they have to read something on their own, it is a good idea to read the first paragraph to them whilst they look at the text. From the first paragraph it is usually possible to learn what the whole piece is going to be about. It also establishes the style of writing, such as whether it is humorous or serious, or if there are words in a dialect which might alter the spelling of certain words. If pupils are in a situation where they are choosing their own books to read there is a simple test which can be used to make sure the child does not choose a book which has too many words with which he will have difficulty (otherwise more than half the lesson can be spent going up to ask the words or changing book after book!). In the 'finger test' the child takes a book from the shelf. He opens it at the middle page and begins to read from the top. He places his little finger on the first word he cannot read. He places the ring finger on the next failed word, the middle finger on the next...and so on until all the fingers of one hand are used. If he runs out of fingers on *one* hand before the end of the page the book is too difficult at the moment. Children with specific learning difficulties are such fragile readers it is important that they are not put off by trying to read books that present too much difficulty.

If a book has to be read because it is a set text, it could be made available on tape. Many books have already been taped excellently by established actors. A large range of 'classics' have been recently obtainable from newsagents. These beautifully read texts, which come with a well-illustrated booklet of background information, are an invaluable resource for young people with average ability but specific reading difficulties. The youngster with whom I listened to *Wuthering Heights* on tape has since obtained a copy of the book and is now reading it through again, delighted to recognise the story. Talking books for the visually impaired can also be a good source of materials for examination pupils with reading difficulties.

In one school I visit there are many enthusiastic members of a drama group who welcome the opportunity to read texts on to tape for the special needs department. We have some quite dramatic renderings of the first year science course to which pupils have access when they have to do homework from the textbook. Pupils who need this kind of help bring their own tape into school and a sixth former records what is needed on to it. Sometimes sixth formers who are experiencing some difficulty with greatly increased study demands can benefit from trying out for themselves some of the strategies we use with children with reading difficulties.

There are times, of course, when you want to know that the pupil with reading difficulties is actually using support time for learning to read correctly. There is a valuable suggestion for making sure this is being done in a handbook for those helping adolescent dyslexics (Stirling 1985). The pupil is told to set a quiz of a specified number of questions on what he has just read. When he has finished the teacher takes a few minutes reading through the passage chosen and read by the pupil before being asked the questions. This way the pupil reads carefully because he knows that he must know the answers, but he is not in the position where he risks the failure of being asked questions he cannot answer. This method has been suggested to parents who want to know how they can help their children who have passed the stage where listening to them read each evening is appropriate. A child can be encouraged to prepare a quiz for his parent on the science the child has been set for homework. The parent must be prepared to be undismayed if he or she fails on some of the questions!

It is also important that there is plenty of reading matter available of the kind that motivates young people to read. Scornful though many adults are of the *Readers' Digest* the articles have the advantage of being short and are usually high in human interest. Several reluctant readers of my acquaintance have become engrossed in articles from this and it has given them a starting point for their own writing. Computer magazines and teenage magazines also motivate very reluctant readers. Pupils with specific reading difficulties will only improve their reading skills if they have plenty of practice. For that reason it is important not to be dismissive of reading matter which lacks the beauty and endurance of the classics. If the child can become so engrossed in a story of his football or rock band hero in a newspaper that he cannot hear you calling for his attention, then he must be reading with understanding.

Some children's reading difficulties are so great that they might never read for pleasure but only use reading as a tool. I have yet to meet the pupil who cannot look up the television programmes in the paper, or read a letter or report that concerns himself (unless it has been written in deliberately obscure language).

Strategies for writing difficulties

The child with writing difficulties is often labelled careless or untidy unless he also has significant difficulties in reading and spelling. Since writing is a more creative activity than reading or spelling it is also more complex. Not only are there a variety of different styles of writing for different occasions and audiences but there are fairly rigid rules to be obeyed.

There are two aspects to supporting a child with writing problems. The first is to help the pupil to make his work look pleasant and inviting to read. One of the pupils whom I support writes excellent stories where he keeps a number of characters acting in a breath-taking manner until the end of the story, but unless he is beside you it will take a couple of hours to decipher the story. He now has a laptop computer. He dictates his story on to tape and then listens to it, one sentence at a time, through his Walkman, and types it out. He finishes by using the spell checker just before he prints out. He is handing in some of the best work in the class. Of course he will have to write his GCSE examination by hand, and so we are working at actual 'penmanship' at the same time. When he has to write notes in his science or geography book he dictates them to the support teacher, the lab technician, the class teacher or a helper from the sixth form. His amanuensis writes them in pencil in a simple but flowing style which is taught by many dyslexia tutors. At home he must carefully write over the pencil marks, beginning where the first letter begins and keeping the flow of the word. Ideally he should say the word as he writes it. This method has been used with a number of pupils who have been so pleased with the way their over-writing looks in their books that they have been weaned off the help and have adopted this style, and, because of the way in which the letters are linked, this style of writing also serves to reinforce spelling rules.

The SENCO in a selective boys' school, where a number of boys arrive with writing difficulties, recommends that they start off by writing on alternate lines. Not only does this immediately make the writing easier for the teacher to read but it gives the work a less cluttered appearance. Also many children with spelling difficulties as well as writing difficulties write with minuscule letters that are barely visible to the human eye. By using alternate lines, they have to develop a larger style of writing. I imagine a further advantage would be that a pupil will reach the end of the book earlier; and, if an improvement has been made, the old book can soon be discarded, and there is an incentive to make a new start in the fresh book. The boys decide for himself when they are ready to use all the lines and they might do this in some subjects before others. It is important that secondary pupils with any specific kind of learning difficulty have some kind of control over the strategies they are using.

Sometimes it is not just the penmanship that is difficult for the pupil. He also has difficulty with constructing sentences and paragraphs. It is important for the pupil to realise that a series of short sentences is preferable to long complex ones. A support teacher can help to check whether there is a verb in each sentence and whether the addition of an adjective or adverb would make the sentence more meaningful. She can also help with the understanding of paragraphs as a group of sentences grouped because of their relationship with each other. Learning to plan an essay at an early stage in secondary school life is very important for these children if they are to receive a grade in English which reflects their general ability.

The English GCSE examination is a great worry for those with reading or writing difficulties. The choice of essay titles is a very important one. Pupils with these difficulties should have help with being able to determine which title will put them at least disadvantage. An essay where the beginning or end of the story is given is very difficult to do well in as the style and story have been predetermined and might not be a style familiar to the pupil. An essay depending on description is also a risk for those who have difficulty with remembering and spelling varied vocabulary. Probably an essay which depends on providing opinions is the safest to attempt. Advice should be given on preparing by jotting down ideas and facts before starting the essay. From Year 7 any help given with drafting and redrafting will be an investment for the time of examinations.

A personal laptop computer can be a tremendous help if the child is supported in learning to use it when it is provided. However there is a danger that too often pupils who know that this is a recommendation on their statement look forward to it in joyful anticipation because they believe it will solve all their difficulties. An example of this was Anna. Anna was a fourteen-year-old girl with not only really severe reading, writing and spelling difficulties but also extremely well-developed techniques for avoiding putting pen to paper. She was given a very sophisticated word processor as part of sponsorship from a local firm and proudly carried her machine, the envy of her classmates, to all her lessons. Unfortunately one of the problems with her writing was that she had never sorted out the difference between upper case and lower case letters, and so often the middle letters in her words were upper case since she scattered capitals in a totally random fashion. Her inaugural session with the word processor could have provided the motivation for her to learn the function of upper case letters. However, she simply did everything in upper case or lower case, depending on how the shift key was initially set. She also could have benefited from the built in spell checker but since she had never come across the word 'edit' (and to her consult dictionary meant just that, and she had never found dictionaries much help), she soon lost enthusiasm for the machine. When the ink started to leak, she was told to take it to the office to be repaired. I have not seen her with it since, but it certainly did not provide the help for which she had hoped; and I am sure she felt some sense of failure that even with this miracle machine she could not produce good work.

In another school there is a policy of planning the introduction of the laptop computer to the child. The child is not lent the machine until there is someone in the room, such as a support teacher or a sixth former, who has time to supervise the pupil through the first couple of pieces of work and explain how the spell checker works. At first a computer is lent on a trial basis, and it is carefully evaluated by the teachers and the pupil. Because of the difficulty of carrying extra luggage, the smallest laptops possible which have full-size keyboards are used, and access to a shared printer is arranged. If the introduction goes well and the pupil is obviously benefiting from the use of the computer then one will be allocated, and sometimes even a portable printer that can be taken home for homework is provided.

A laptop is only of value to a child with writing difficulties if functions such as 'cut and paste', 'edit' and 'move file' are understood. Many children with specific learning difficulties have already suffered years of frustration, and it is important that what is meant to help them does not leave them with another experience of failure.

Strategies for spelling difficulties

Words to help with spelling should be immediately entered into a little book which is easy to refer to. Often the support teacher needs to enter the word while the pupil is putting it into his classwork. At the beginning of the lesson, while the class is settling, it can be useful to look through what has been done in the pupil's book since your last support with him, and comment on any spelling error as you put the correct version in his book. It has to be his decision whether he changes the spelling in the work already done, but if his specific learning difficulties are the reason for which he has been allocated support, I would not see this as cheating in any way.

When a pupil turns to me to ask for a word, after I have spelt it I often say it a few times both as it is spelt and in its correct pronunciation as I find that pupils can often spell words that they have learned to mispronounce, especially those with a 'gh' in the middle. Because so many pupils make mistakes by missing out syllables, I stress the importance of reading back the work.

There are some pupils who are motivated enough to use a commercially produced spell checker very effectively. Spell checkers have improved greatly and the latest Franklin one can recognise some of the more bizarre spellings such as 'nolij' for 'knowledge', 'creecher' for 'creature' and 'shofer' for 'chauffeur'. Those who have laptop computers usually have software with a spell checker, but again, they must have the motivation and the understanding to use this. There is also a Spelling Checklist/Dictionary for Dyslexics (Stirling 1985) which is very useful and easy to use in the classroom.

It is difficult to actually teach spelling whilst supporting in a science or geography lesson but, in common with most support, it is often a matter of trying to increase an adolescent's confidence in his own ability to find the resources to help himself. Frequently, rather than spelling the word that is requested, it is better to ask the child what does he think the first letter will be? what is the sound that this is linked to? are there other sounds before the end? and how does it end? At each stage prompting can help the child discover not only the spelling but the rule, or the exception, as the case may be. One of the very satisfying aspects of supporting specific learning difficulties in secondary classrooms is that the children are old enough to discuss the strategies they are using to overcome their difficulties, and sometimes they can be the ones who make suggestions. The skill of the support teacher is in motivating the children to want to develop the means to take control of their own learning. If the person supporting is merely going to spell words for them in class, there seems little point in paying the salary of a qualified teacher! Rather, the teacher should be mediating the learning and boosting the pupil's confidence in his ability to manage his own problems.

Strategies for improving memory

Both short-term and long-term memory is seen as a vital element in specific learning difficulties. There is a theory (Morrison et al. 1977) that 'dyslexics' hold images in the mind for a shorter time than pupils without these difficulties. Farnham-Diggory (1978) suggests that the act of remembering is not a passive one, and it is necessary to have programmes for remembering that involve 'attention, rehearsal and other kinds of information management'. The classic way of teaching dyslexic pupils, and indeed other pupils also, to learn spellings is to instruct them to: look, cover, try, look; and if you do not succeed do this again. This method is also used to learn mathematical formulae and facts from other subjects and also modern language vocabulary.

The multi-sensory programmes that were mentioned earlier all take into account memory difficulties. A favourite maxim of the British Dyslexia Association is: *If I hear I forget, If I see I remember, if I touch I understand.*

Some children with specific learning difficulties find that they remember best if they repeat things over and over again to themselves as soon as they have been told. An example of this is the young man who repeated his homework over and over to himself as his writing was so bad he knew neither he nor his mother would be able to read it when he arrived home. When, at the age of fourteen, he started to learn to skate, he amazed his coaches by remembering everything he had been taught from lesson to lesson. He had lessons on a Saturday and a Wednesday. Immediately after each lesson he would do two or three total reruns of it, repeating everything the teacher had said. He often ran through the dialogue again in the car on the way home. He did not leave the ice until he was happy that he had internalised the lesson. Within five years he was in the British Ice Dance Squad, where he used the same method to memorise the complicated steps and patterns of all the international compulsory ice dances. People often remarked on how well he would have done if he had started skating at an earlier age; but I doubt he would have achieved anywhere near his present success as he did not have the confidence in his ability early on to take charge of his own learning.

Some children with a memory problem feel that there is nothing that they can do about it. However, it is possible to devise discreet methods of prompting the memory. I am sorry that some teachers feel constrained to punish pupils who use the back of their hand as an impromptu notebook (there is no danger unless there is an open wound or Indian ink is used). Pupils constantly ask me about the reminders on the back of my left hand and are intrigued that a cluster of single letters can contain a myriad of reminders. From the stage of needing to write whole word reminders, I try to wean pupils to needing the first letter of each word to be remembered. I encourage them to keep a few pocket or purse size pieces of paper on them so that they can record anything they need to remember. There is also a small, inexpensive recording machine available that will hold about five minutes worth of recorded messages and fit into a blazer pocket. This retails at about £10, but might be well worth buying for an upper secondary student who still has difficulty in recording basic notes about his homework.

Strategies for improving organisational skills

I mentioned thinking skills in the previous chapter on moderate learning difficulties. A methodical course of thinking skills would certainly benefit most dyslexic children. A number of the groups that have grown up around the country to study and do research on the outcome of thinking skills training are also linked with organisations catering for the needs of children with specific learning difficulties. A manufacturer in Kent, Bowater Scott, is so convinced of the effectiveness of thinking skills training in improving the general level of everyone's ability that they have put quite generous sponsorship into those promoting thinking skills in Kent. All young people joining the firm do a course of thinking skills as part of their induction process. Again, one of the values of thinking skills is that it encourages students to think about their own methods of thinking (meta-cognition) and by doing this to be able to exercise more control over the efficiency of their thinking. Children with specific learning difficulties are rarely able to succeed when they attack a task in an impulsive or random way. The thinking skills movement was inspired by those who saw a need to prevent children, especially those who had had an unsettled early life, from doing everything in a totally haphazard and unplanned way. It was to help them to internalise a sense of order and purpose in tasks. Most programmes that succeed with dyslexics contain these elements.

Support teachers in the classroom, especially in the earlier years of secondary education, need to help their protégées with developing a ritual for setting out their work neatly. Help given early on can increase confidence as the work is satisfying to look at. This is an area where the support teacher really needs to consult the class teacher to find out what will be required throughout the year. It is, of course, easier in a school where all children carry a small book, known as a diary or journal, where they note down their homework, teachers write in messages to the home, and parents sign at regular intervals, acknowledging they have seen it. If there is also a policy about how the date is written and widths of margins, etc., it is worth clipping a model headed page into the diary or journal that the child carries so that he can quickly look at it before putting pen to paper.

The diary or journal will be a lifeline between the child with specific learning difficulties, the school and the parents. The support teacher can use time before and after a lesson making sure that the diary is up-to-date, that the child is using the right page and has not accidentally skipped a day, a week, a month or even a term. Some children consistently forget P.E., and technology equipment, and when you look in their diaries you find entries made at random. I liked the idea of one teacher who gave each child a rubber band to mark the page in the diary (placed over the pages between the front or back cover and the right page). Each Monday morning this teacher checks that everyone is on the right page. Although there is a fair bit of twanging of rubber bands, it does help those who find self organisation difficult.

With younger children, a support teacher can sometimes help by going through the child's school bag (in his presence, of course, and with his permission) and collecting the equipment, notes, etc. that have gathered in the bottom. If it is a bag with a number of separate compartments the support teacher can talk through with the child how he can set aside each area for a different purpose. If this is done in the first weeks of the first year it can start a habit which will stand the child in good stead throughout his school life. A child who has poor organisational skills might well come from a home where a parent also has similar difficulties. It is acknowledged that reading, writing and spelling difficulties can run in families but not so often suggested that memory and organisational difficulties might also.

Children with organisational difficulties will need a great deal of support early in their secondary school careers but this should not be support which takes over the responsibility for remembering. Any help given should be discussed and the child should be asked to suggest strategies that he might use to help himself. Sometimes going around with a class mate who is well-organised and knows the timetable and what is needed for each lesson can help greatly during the first half term, as long as the pupil with special needs does not become dependent, but uses this as a temporary crutch.

In the higher forms, students with organisational difficulties will need extra support a few weeks before examinations and when assignments are due in. It will be important for them to compile a study plan and a time management plan. Although they might need considerable help initially this should be gradually weaned away, especially if the student is thinking of going on to further or higher education.

The importance of preserving self-esteem

It is unfortunate that, in order to obtain extra resources for support in school, the learning and ability deficits of the child have to be emphasised. The important fact about pupils with specific learning difficulties is that their learning difficulties are specific and not 'across the board', as are those of the child with moderate learning difficulties. Children, and their parents, are often surprised when I point out to them that there are more things that the pupils can do than that they cannot do. This is important because, from the start, they must learn to use those strengths to compensate and devise strategies for overcoming the areas of difficulty.

For many parents, it is a terrible blow to learn that their children have serious learning difficulties. The children will have heard their parents expressing their concern and might pick up a certain hopelessness from them. This is confirmed when they know they have statements of special needs and even an extra teacher to work with them in some lessons. It is important for their self-esteem that it is a partnership between the children with the learning difficulties and the support teacher. When sitting with these children in the classroom it is important for the support teacher to treat them as intelligent human beings with their own ability to reason, then they might feel confident enough to let others in the group work out strategies with them to overcome their difficulties.

I taught one adolescent who was convinced that he would never be able to do anything as he was 'dyslexic'. His parents were very involved in the local dyslexia association and had tried very hard to enlist the help of as many experts as possible to help him. He had no confidence in his own ability to do anything. However, when he arrived in the science lab at his new secondary school it was not immediately evident to anyone that he had a problem since early lessons were oral and mainly about lab safety and how experiments should be done. He had plenty of common sense and was often ahead of the others in answering. When experiments were started, he was often the one with the best ideas on how a theory could be tested and validated. Unfortunately, it was not possible to read what he had written, if indeed he wrote anything down. Often when told to write he would delay as long as possible and then stop when he reached the first word he was not sure about spelling. When I was supporting him he dictated his notes to me, I wrote them in pencil and he wrote over them. This way he gained confidence with writing and began to realise that his ability to spell was improving. Fortunately, when the boys had to chose a partner with whom to work, several offered to work with him as he had good ideas. He wisely chose a partner who was extremely neat and tidy, although lacking in flair and originality. They made a good partnership and Robert's self-esteem increased so much from being in this partnership, especially as he was able to help his partner as much as his partner helped him.

This kind of arrangement, which exploits the talents of all, can often happen in lessons such as Science, Technology, Geography and History, but is more difficult in Modern Languages. Although some pupils with specific learning difficulties have an excellent ear for oral work most have difficulty with the reading, writing and spelling of a foreign language. French seems to cause more problems than German or Spanish because of the discrepancy (to English students) between how the word is written and how it is pronounced. It is important that teachers of modern languages are aware of the difficulties experienced by pupils so that they do not over-emphasise the written work. It often helps to point out to children with difficulties that it is more likely that they will be called upon to speak or listen to the foreign language than that they will have to read or write it. Fortunately the National Curriculum puts as much emphasis on speaking and listening as on reading and writing.

It is of paramount importance that any support given is geared towards total independence and that the students are always aware that it is their own strengths upon which they are building.

Choices after school

It is also important that the child with specific learning difficulties does not see the choice of an academic path after school as the only way to gain success. Although some pupils with difficulties achieve 'A' Level passes, 'A' Level puts tremendous pressure on many young people who have not had difficulties. Young people with specific learning difficulties will need considerable professional support in selecting the right pathway to follow after school.

For young people who have always had considerably more difficulty than their peers in reading and writing, but have good cognitive and oral skills, the newly formulated GNVQ (General National Vocational Qualification) courses could be very suitable. These courses will be available in Colleges of Further Education and some Sixth Forms, and the emphasis is on the kind of thinking, recording, communication and reference to sources that would be required in the work place. They replace the more familiar BTEC courses. At higher levels these courses will be demanding of time and planning, and will have the rigour of 'A' Level courses but without the demands for a very high level of literacy. There will also be a requirement to be able to function as the member of a team with a specific task to do, within a certain time. These courses will not be an easy option, and employers will be aware of what each level of achievement means. They will, at their higher levels, be an alternative entry requirement for university.

Because of the rigour of these courses, which are already being dubbed 'vocational 'A' Levels', they will not be suitable for all school leavers. Some will find NVQs (National Vocational Qualification), the vocational qualifications which are based in the work-place, much more suitable. These qualifications validate practical competencies in a very systematic way.

It is important that whatever the dyslexic school leavers do after school, it is what they really want and not undertaken just to satisfy what others think they should do. Because of their difficulties, these pupils will have to be really motivated if their choices involve further study, since this will always entail more effort. The young man who skates hated modern languages at school but, with the possibility of training and competing in France and Germany, he is eagerly brushing up his skills in French and German and practising conversation on anyone who can respond. It is absolutely vital to focus on the young person's strengths when supporting them through the transition from school to further education or work.

CHAPTER 5
Supporting the 'impossible child' in the classroom

Children with the kind of difficulties described in the last two chapters could well be described to the support teacher as presenting behaviour problems. The interface between behavioural difficulties and learning difficulties is so narrow that the former is often used to cover the latter. Although children with bad behaviour pose a different problem in class to those with learning difficulties only, it is important to home in on the child's learning first. For very often bad behaviour is an escape for the child who never has any success with his school work, or who finds reading and following instructions almost impossible.

The boy described here will be familiar to many teachers:

> That boy's got problems with his reading, his comprehension, in getting things together enough to get them down on paper...This boy not only needs learning support, he needs one-to-one to keep him at it. He takes advantage. It's not just learning support, it's behavioural support. Really I am not sure that dire cases like this should be in mainstream.

He is fairly typical of the children who are often allocated support in the mainstream school, and the child in question could well be a girl! It is their tendency to disrupt the class and affect the quality of teaching that causes as much concern as their own learning difficulty. It is also a common complaint that such children need constant attention in 'getting things together' and in 'keeping at it'. They also usually have well-honed avoidance techniques, which can delay the work of all the pupils in the class.

Depressed and sad children might have just as much need of the support of an extra adult in the classroom in order to reach their full potential; but if they sit quietly picking at their fingers, or staring out of the window, they are much less likely to attract enough attention to receive the help they undoubtedly need. However, fortunately, they might have the courage to 'refer' themselves to the receptive support teacher as she has time to listen to them. This is rarely the case with children presenting disruptive behaviour.

Sometimes bad behaviour might be the reaction of the child who is being under-extended and no longer finds any challenge in the classroom. Unfortunately children, especially boys, have quite cruel names for those of their number who excel and request more challenging work, and so the very able child might become the class-clown during the lesson whilst handing in well executed homework, despite giving the appearance of not having paid attention during the lesson. The SENCO in a selective school made this comment:

> There are a few very clever boys who are failed by the curriculum. There are a few boys at the upper end of the school who channel their high ability into getting into trouble, lots of trouble. When they decide to do something wrong it really is quite a trouble to us because they have the intelligence to really annoy us.

The child who is described as 'impossible' by teachers is the one who crosses the limits which few children dare to challenge. Very often teachers complain for many months about these pupils and are asked to review their own skills. Often it is only when the pupil finally takes on a member of the senior management team that meetings are held and there is concern that this child should be either brought under control or excluded. Whole school systems of yellow and red cards, followed up by incident reports, can sometimes be successful in initiating intervention for such children as this before they have the opportunity to affect the education of other children too severely. Nevertheless the behaviour of some pupils is totally unaffected by the most carefully thought out system of sanctions, and yet teachers are expected to teach them in a class of pupils, some of whom are eager to learn but others of whom are very willing to be distracted by the disruptive pupil.

Although we are all only too aware of the features of present day society which can cause this kind of behaviour in a pupil, unfortunately we are not in a position to change society; but we may well be able to protect the education of the rest of the class.

Support in the classroom

The teacher who is asked to support a child with behavioural difficulties in the classroom has a very different assignment from the teacher who knows what aspect of learning is to be remediated. If the children have reached the stage of having statements in which they are described as needing intervention to remediate their behaviour rather than their learning, one can assume that they have exhausted the complete 'in-house' system of sanctions. However, the fact that you are in the classroom to solve these children's difficulties will have given the teacher high hopes of your ability to do this.

Initially, until you understand the dynamics of the class, your role may well be a reactive one of keeping these pupils on task when there is work to be done, of trying to keep them quiet whilst the teacher is delivering instruction, and preventing disruption of the pupils nearby before it has time to take place. If this is not seen to be happening, the class-teacher might wonder why you are there at all! If you are too obvious in what you are doing, the pupils might see you as issuing a challenge to them. If you give them quiet instructions which they promptly defy, it can be difficult to decide whether to follow through and insist on obedience, with the risk that this might cause a disturbance in class, or whether to quietly ignore them at risk of letting them feel they can play games with you. Ideally you should have time to liaise with the teacher so that you can both discuss these possibilities. Once you have become familiar with the dynamics in a particular classroom you can begin to set some aims for the pupils and, with the teacher's support, offer some kind of reward for achieving those aims. Until now the pupil has often been rewarded for his behaviour with the approbation of his peers and the feeling of his own powerfulness. Intervention will have to recognise his need to be in control, while turning this control into a positive advantage. If the aim is to complete a given piece of work within a time-limit, the child should know exactly what is expected, how long he has and what the reward will be.

When the children enter into this kind of contract it may quickly become evident that one of the reasons for the disruptive behaviour was to avoid work since work which others complete fairly easily poses difficulties for our 'impossible child'. This might be the first time for two or more years that these pupils have been on task long enough for a teacher to realise that they have a learning difficulty. However to comment immediately on this difficulty could well provoke anger, denial and further avoidance behaviour. It may well be best to suggest that you give them some help at this stage with the work since you are there in any case. For example, if the task is to fill in a work sheet you can say, 'Let's see if we can get this out of the way quickly. Shall I read the questions and you give me the answers? Do you want to write them down or shall I? Shall I do them in pencil so you can write over them later? Read them back to me so I know you can read my writing.' A similar approach could be used for making notes or writing up an experiment. Having defined the support that you are offering, in agreement with the teacher, you have the advantage of being able to concentrate your efforts on making sure this section of learning is covered. Class-teachers rarely have the opportunity in a busy, mixed-ability class, to focus on the difficulties of one child.

As you become more familiar with the children and the working of their classes, you will be able to plan ahead areas of work which you can tackle with these pupils. There may well be others in the class, with similar needs, who will refer themselves to you when they see what you are doing. The children you are supporting will almost certainly prefer to be working as a group. As long as the children you have been directed to support have the help they need, the presence of self-referred pupils in the group will be encouraging. If they have really negative feelings about acknowledging their own difficulties they will welcome the presence of others to ask the questions they would like to ask themselves, even though they might pour scorn on the person who asks.

If the support of these children turns out to be so easily productive, you are indeed lucky – although I have experienced several cases where, once learning difficulties were discovered, it was possible to work in this way. In three cases they were children of at least average ability who had a specific difficulty with actually heading the work and starting. Others had spelling and writing difficulties also, and initially tore up their work whenever a mistake was noted. One of the main tasks of the support teacher was to draw a second set of very light guidelines on each page to help to keep the writing even and to be ready to offer to spell any word which was difficult.

Where this support has been more difficult is where the pupil is having difficulty in grasping any of the work that is being taught. In a busy class, if there is no match between the children's ability and the work being taught, the support teacher has often to start by helping the pupils directly to produce the work which they can hand in, regardless of whether they understand it or not. Only when the children have had some experience of success, and the two teachers can discuss the difficulties, is the planning of individual programmes possible.

Although differentiation has been spoken about in schools for many years – and good teachers were practising it in their classrooms long before the word to define it entered the growing special needs lexicon – there are many situations where it is difficult to put into action. Take the modern language class of thirty pupils, where each pupil works towards a set assessment each half term during their 90 minutes a week of language lessons. There is bound to be a need to teach the class as a whole and the teacher has this situation replicated up to nine times each week. The acting out, disruptive child is a particular problem in modern language lessons as any individual work is going to entail pupils working in pairs, often orally. This gives the child who lacks motivation or confidence, and has learnt to avoid failure with noisy behaviour, a licence to disrupt the work of the class.

There are also times when these children with scant regard for the effect they have on others cause great anxiety in lessons. Indeed, there are certain children who are not welcome in a science lab or a technology workshop unless there is a support teacher there to make sure that the safety of the rest of the class, as well as the individual, is not put at risk. These are situations where it is sometimes valuable to support disruptive members of the class, for at least part of the lesson, outside the classroom, so it is to this we now turn.

Support outside the classroom

Even in schools where there are misgivings about any child receiving support outside the classroom, the time often comes when it is agreed to attempt to help a child presenting behavioural problems in this way. As one very experienced SENCO remarked:

> There are some teachers who would like the child withdrawn to give them all a breather...The behavioural ones are linked with learning difficulties. I think we have some very entrenched learning difficulties.

Sometimes a period of withdrawal support gives pupils an opportunity to produce coursework of which they can be proud. It is sometimes difficult for pupils, to whom others look for entertainment and relief from boredom, to change in class unless they have some other way to build their self-esteem. Unless such pupils have some experience of recognisable success they have little invested in changing their ways. Often they only realise the seriousness of their misbehaviour when they have actually reached the stage of being excluded from school.

One such child was a girl called Tracey, whom I supported, who was awaiting a place at the local school for pupils with emotional and behavioural difficulties. In a school which was diametrically opposed to withdrawal, I was asked to withdraw her from her two modern language lessons each week and do whatever I could with her. I attempted to continue the language work with her, but her anger and sense of failure were so great that these initial sessions were totally unproductive. I was not prepared to waste this valuable time each week so I began by capitalising on what I knew she cared about. From the black varnish on her nails and her deathly white make-up, it was easy to see that she was a follower of the 'Gothic cult', adhered to by so many teenagers at that time. I asked her about it and enlisted her help in writing an informative guide for the parents and teachers on 'Gothics'. She did this with great enthusiasm and, for the first time in two years, started taking tasks home. She enjoyed seeing her work growing and used some lunch-times to type it out. She started showing it to some of her teachers and receiving positive feedback from them. Her English teacher was particularly fulsome in her praise for what had been achieved and Tracey began to work with equal enthusiasm in her English lessons.

Some teachers felt that I was pandering too much to Tracey's own interests. I was certainly in a very privileged position, compared to them, to do this. However she was so entrenched in her avoidance of what she felt she could not do that, with all my experience, I could find no other way of motivating her. She was interested to hear that there were Gothics in other European countries who followed the same fashions and listened to the same music. At this time I suggested that it might be easier for me to continue to withdraw her from French and German if we at least tried to do some modern language work.

We settled into a pattern of doing tasks set by the language teacher first and using the time left over to continue with the other work. Tracey was eager to complete the work so that she could continue with her own interest, and enjoyed writing some sentences in her project in French and German as well as English.

I cannot claim that she became a model pupil, but there were certainly less complaints about her behaviour. She had the confidence to start pieces of work and take them home to finish for homework. This intervention had a favourable effect on any work that she could illustrate, and the science and geography teachers gave her encouragement even though her ornate diagrams sometimes missed the point of the lesson. She also had much more confidence in language lessons and no longer disturbed every lesson by asking loudly why she had to learn this language which she would never use. The success of this intervention could not have been achieved without the 'tongue in cheek' generosity of some of her teachers who were not quite sure why but knew they needed to encourage her.

In other cases where I have taken pupils with behavioural problems out of the classroom, the improvement in attitude has occurred after a period of quietly looking through all the unfinished or aborted work of the week and deciding which pieces of work will be salvaged during this session. When one withdraws a child with learning difficulties from the curriculum it is totally appropriate to try to cover some concepts presented in the work being done by the rest of the class. With a child who has emotional and behavioural difficulties, however, if you dig your heels in and insist on this you might well trigger a replication of the behaviour in the classroom and waste valuable time trying to prove that you can make the child do what you want. I usually start by finding out which of the pieces of work that has to be submitted in the next few days, is nearest to completion. Sometimes the pupil is very relieved to find that this can be completed in the first few minutes of the session. Sometimes a little 'cosmetic' work has to be done. Essential tools of a support teacher are cellotape, tippex, a good pencil and ink rubber, a ruler and a red pen. The latter is not for marking purposes but because so many pupils seem to obtain great pleasure from handing in their work with all headings underlined with a double red line. At this stage of support the aim is to build self-esteem and make the pupil feel pleased with his work.

If the pupil's teachers will agree initially to other work being completed during the period of withdrawal, it is often possible to give the pupil the opportunity of favourable feedback and success in a number of lessons. This will be spoilt if any teacher feels that this kind of help is cheating and denounces the help that the child has received. For this reason, liaison with all the teachers concerned with this child is essential, even if it is only achieved by a photocopied note in a pigeon hole, introducing yourself and saying how you would like to work and inviting comments before you start.

Once the initial period of this kind of support has passed it might be possible to focus the work during this period more securely on the curriculum being covered by the rest of the teaching group. This should be done before the pupil can be reintegrated into the lesson. If the withdrawal has been from this lesson because this has been the lesson where the pupil has presented the most problems, it will be important that both the pupil and the teacher are confident about the child's return. The pupil must be armed with some hope of success, and the teacher must have some optimism about the reintegration.

Sometimes withdrawal periods are used for counselling pupils. If the child has long-standing emotional problems and the support teacher is a skilled and experienced counsellor, this can be extremely valuable. However, if this is seen by the child as an opportunity to leave the class and have a cosy chat with a special adult who makes him feel good without making any demands on him to change, he, and his teachers, can feel let down at the end of the arrangement. If this form of support is given, it is important that targets for change are negotiated and are known by the children concerned, their teachers and, possibly, the parents. Unfortunately many children have to endure much more suffering and injustice than their teachers will ever understand. However, we are patronising them and giving them unrealistic hopes for the future if we pretend that the adult world they face will be less demanding than that for which we are preparing other young people. I sincerely hope that schools will eventually realise the value of counselling for some pupils. Ideally children who need this service should have access to it during lunch-times and before and after school.

As support teachers, significant in the education of children with special needs, we will have the opportunity to take part in the regular reviews of our pupils' progress. If we feel that they are in need of professional counselling, or even the protection of social services, we shall have the opportunity to voice this. Meanwhile, our task is to support their educational needs and work in collaboration with their subject teachers and form tutors. Nevertheless, we might have a role to play in liaison between the school and the family if the school sees this as being appropriate. I would hesitate to initiate any involvement with the family without the blessing of the senior management team at the school.

Support with the child's family

In my experience only one family of pupils I was supporting has avoided contact with me, and this was achieved by pretending to be out whenever I called on prearranged visits. I respected their feelings, but wished they had felt able to simply say they did not wish for my involvement. A more common experience, in contrast, has been having to limit my visits to one or two a term and state firmly at the beginning how long I shall be staying.

If I am discussing a child's behaviour with parents or other significant adults (grandparents, older siblings, foster parents) I like the child to be present. I do this partly to preserve the relationship of trust which I have already built up with the child, and partly because I do not want to be used against the child in my absence. Early in my career I learned that when I spoke to the parents and carers of diffi-cult children without the child present, as many of us used to on parents' evenings, words would be put into my mouth in an attempt to control the youngsters. Later I have had to face angry youngsters whose parents had told them that I had suspected them of taking drugs, having sex, going to bed too late, and stealing money at home. Although there was no truth in these allegations my denials had a hollow ring.

However, even if the child is not present, a short visit can still be a useful opportunity to discuss perspectives of education and hopes and fears for the future. Very often you find that a family, which initially presents an aggressive front has members who are seriously lacking in self-esteem. Parents will often admit to the strategies they used to avoid being 'shown up' in class and that their own experi-ence of school was unhappy. If you profess admiration for the fact that they now run a successful business or workshop, or a mother is coping with two or three other children as well as the child you support, they are often amazed that you can recognise their skills or talents. I recently visited a home only to find that the mother was a girl whom I had taught in a unit for disruptive adolescents I had run for some years. Susan, at 30, was coping with her own three chil-dren, the first of whom had been conceived before she left school, and with two handicapped stepchildren of her second husband as well as a young baby. Her thirteen-year-old whom I supported was always in immaculate uniform at the start of the day and must have had a clean shirt every day. Susan welcomed an opportunity to talk about the family and understood the need to build up the self-esteem of her two eldest children.

Often when the withdrawal support has been so successful that it is due to be phased out, the family can have a very important role in helping the child to organise his work and make sure that all the equipment he needs is available. Many children are constantly given detentions for incomplete homework when they do not have the facilities at home to do it. Sometimes a home visit is valuable in identifying an area of the home that can be cleared to make room for homework. In a chaotic home, help in deciding on a routine to ensure equipment is brought to school on the day it is needed, is usually accepted with good grace. Sometimes it is evident that the mother, or the main care-giver in the home, is in a depressed state and it would be unfair to add to the burden by such demands. It is then important that the child's teachers are aware of the situation.

An example of this is the fourteen-year-old who was in constant trouble about the state of her uniform and her failure to return messages to school and have her weekly journal signed. The staff had initially been understanding when they learned that the girl's forty-year-old mother had died of cancer but they lost patience when, a year later, the family still did not seem to be coping. They did not realise that the girl's father was 75 years old, blind and had lost one arm in the war. In addition to this, the family home was under constant attack by young burglars whilst Julia was at school, so she was often missing school in order to defend their property. As so often happens, much of the anger Julia felt about the sudden death of her mother, a very vivacious woman, and her home situation was taken out on her teachers at school. Support in this case was to help her to understand what was happening, and what she was doing to alienate her teachers, and to inform the appropriate people at school so that they could alert social services.

It is important that when you visit homes, the children presenting behavioural problems do not feel that you are ganging up with their parents against them. As a support teacher you are in a very privileged position because you see the children in school. Unless it is the specific purpose of the home visit, this is not the time to tell tales about what happens in the classroom. If the child decides to introduce an incident into the conversation, you can confirm the facts and discuss it; but a home visit is best used as an opportunity for the child to see you and his parents as a partnership concerned with helping him to cope at school. As an advocate for that particular child you are representing the special needs department at the school and forging links between the school and the family.

Support in relation to the teacher who is facing challenging behaviour

The most stressful aspect of a teacher's life is having to teach a class where much of the time is spent dealing with disciplinary matters. In the Summary of the Elton Report (1989) this statement is made:

> Press comments have tended to concentrate on attacks by pupils on teachers. Our evidence indicates that attacks are rare in schools in England and Wales. We also see that teachers do not see attacks as their

major problem...Teachers in our survey were most concerned about the cumulative effect of disruption to their lessons caused by relatively trivial but persistent misbehaviour. (Summary, para.3, p.11)

A little further on the same page it states:

...even in well run schools minor disruption seems to be a problem. The relatively trivial incidents which most concern teachers make it harder for teachers to teach and pupils to learn. (para. 5)

In the few years since the publication of this report, behaviour problems have been attributed to the fact that many subject teachers have been bound by law to deliver an assessment-led curriculum. Added to this there has been tremendous pressure from senior management teams who are anxious about the school's place in the published league tables.

More helpfully in this context, however, the recommendation for behaviour support teams to be set up has also been implemented. However, each team can only work with a handful of pupils in each school. This work often takes the form of counselling the difficult child outside the classroom and sitting beside the pupil in the classroom and helping him with his work. At this stage an attempt is made to avoid having the child formally statemented. However, if the pupil already has a statement, this support is more likely to be provided by an 'all-purpose' support teacher or a classroom assistant.

We all know how pleasant and interesting even the most difficult children can be when we have the opportunity to give them some individual attention. When we are singing the praises of these pupils to the subject teacher, who has had to deal with them in a class of thirty, it is important to recognise that we realise that we have been in a privileged position. However much the subject teacher has wanted to have some kind of relief from the constant interruptions that one child can make in a class, he or she will often feel some sense of failure for not managing alone.

It is important that the support teacher recognises the difference between the task of the teacher of the whole class and his or her task with that one child. It is important to listen carefully to what the subject specialists say about the child and to show by your questions that you have been listening. Although you may feel tempted to tell a colleague about the success you have just experienced in persuading the child to do his work, or in realising that the pupil is now motivated to work for you, this might be best shared with another support teacher rather than one who has still had to battle with the twenty-nine left over. However if the teacher has made a suggestion of some work, or a strategy to try, let him or her know if it was successful. Use the time when you are working with the child in a one-to-one situation to discuss what goes wrong in the classroom and to negotiate targets for improvement in aspects of behaviour. It should be clear that the teachers will be told about these targets and that you will wish to know to what extent they are being met.

Some children initially enjoy the individual attention so much that they are afraid of improving in case they lose this. I explain that there is no point in working like this unless they are going to use the sessions well, and explain that if they do not reach their targets this way of working is not right for them. It is probably best to make these targets as specific as possible, ('to address teachers politely' is better than 'to behave well') and only one or two at a time. It is also important not to set too ambitious targets to begin with. For example, Paul, a lively thirteen-year-old, was constantly out of his seat and had the habit of shouting across the room. For half a term it was agreed that he would spend one of his two French lessons a week outside the classroom. During this withdrawal period part of the time was spent on improving his French and the rest spent negotiating behavioural targets.

We tackled the shouting first as that is what the teacher found the most disruptive in French lessons. Paul shouted out three times in the first lesson after a target had been set. This was much less than usual, and the teacher commented favourably as he left the room. The following lesson he only shouted across the room once. However, when the target concerned staying in his seat, he regressed on the shouting as previously he had often gone to the person he wanted to talk to. After a discussion about why he needed to communicate with his friends, even during a short French lesson, Paul agreed that he needed to have more control over this as it was his impulsiveness which was causing most of his trouble. Sometimes when he shouted out it was because he felt that if he put his hand up to answer he should be selected to respond, and if he was not he had the right to shout out. He did reluctantly agree that, in a large class one had to take turns. However, a tactful word with the teacher meant that, while he was battling to bring his own behaviour under control, he was allowed to answer a little more frequently. During the second half of the term I was in the French lesson. Whilst I was there, not surprisingly, he behaved remarkably well. However, I am told that, although his behaviour was never perfect after this programme, it was much controllable by a quiet word or gesture.

When pupils are withdrawn for behaviour support, it is sometimes found that the work being done in the classroom has not been matched with the pupils' ability. In such cases, when the suitable method of addressing the curriculum for these individuals is found, the support teacher can help by making or tracking down the suitable materials. If it is the case of children who work quickly, and therefore either delay starting work or misbehave when they have finished, a set of open-ended work cards can be used as extension exercises and the work collected in a special folder. In the case of the children who have low attainments, work cards can be made as a substitute for the work which is too difficult for them.

As the new Code of Practice (DfE 1994) is implemented, an increasing number of children should be set Individual Educational Plans (IEPs). I have little doubt that SENCOs will welcome the help of experienced support teachers in drawing up these schedules.

Any rewards given by the support teacher for changed behaviour or individual work will have to be agreed with the rest of the child's teachers, as they will not welcome a child who has been used to being awarded a 'credit' for a far humbler piece of work than is normal. This will be especially difficult if the child throws a tantrum in class because he or she cannot be treated more favourably than the others. However, most children understand the importance of an unruly pupil being helped to behave in a more acceptable way. In my experience the majority of pupils become weary of a classmate who is constantly disturbing their lessons and welcome positive strategies to counter this.

Many schools, both before the recommendations in the Elton Report and since then as a result of the Report, have devised whole-school systems of sanctions which are designed to be consistently applied right across the school. Support teachers are in a prime position to know how these sanctions appear to pupils and whether they are effective. How many times does the support teacher, based near the back of the class and among the pupils, realise that the wrong pupil has been given the detention or that the pupil who has been caught was manipulated by other wilier pupils! Unfortunately the support teachers are rarely involved in meetings about discipline within the school, yet they could have a valuable contribution to make.

School sanctions and how support could modify their use

A common pattern of sanctions seems to involve something like this:

(1) A report is sent to the subject or faculty head for early or 'minor' offences.

(2) If this does not act as a deterrent a report is sent to the head of year.

(3) If the latter is repeated, the head of year puts the pupils on report: a yellow card is carried to each lesson to be marked at the end with G for good, S for satisfactory or U for unsatisfactory, is taken home and returned each morning with the parent's signature. There is no doubt that this card nearly always has an effect during the lessons in which it is carried. The theory is, I presume, that if the pupils realise how much more pleasant life is for them when they are not misbehaving, they will shed the habit during their week on report. There is no doubt that this does sometimes occur, especially with younger pupils who have only recently started to cause concern.

(4) If the misbehaviour recurs, a red card is given, and any U on this will mean automatic referral to a member of the senior management team and the threat of suspension. This also works while the threat of suspension is live. However, some pupils have been the whole way through this kind of system a number of times and are still presenting unacceptable behaviour. Unfortunately, there are rarely the resources necessary to be able to call on the local authority's behavioural support team whenever needed.

Although the report card system works effectively for many it is evident that some children with more entrenched behaviour problems actually enjoy the extra attention which is given when they have a card. In one school I visit, pupils can request to be on report, an admission that they cannot behave without some extrinsic support. A useful role of the support teacher is therefore to help these pupils to control their own behaviour without relying on outside threats. One of the main aims of support in the secondary school is, surely, to lead the pupils to more successful independence in their later lives. Adults who cannot control their behaviour enjoy little freedom or friendship.

Support to close the reality gap

Many pupils who cause constant annoyance and stress in class hotly deny that they have done anything wrong when they are reprimanded. There have been certain pupils whom I have hesitated to reprimand during a lesson as I know that I would immediately be engaged in a futile argument even though I know exactly what I have seen. Mark, the bane of a Year 8 class, was such a pupil. He seemed genuinely amazed when I agreed with the teacher about incidents of misbehaviour. 'But I was only talking!', 'But I only threw it because he asked for it!', 'But I wasn't out of my seat really, I had to put something in the bin' (this said while Mark was at least three metres from his seat). Subsequently, I have kept a record of exactly when he shouted out, chatted to a neighbour, drummed on his desk, left his seat, flicked paper or ink, or made a silly noise. I sat where he could see me putting marks in the columns. He did not actually accuse me of lying, but he did remark that what he was doing was 'nothing really'. It is this kind of flawed reality which forms much of the 'trivial but persistent misbehaviour' which causes teachers such stress. It was difficult to help Mark to see how much he was interfering with the work of his class. In my experience, when pupils like Mark see their behaviour in class on video they are very embarrassed by it, especially when they see their own peers becoming angry. They are usually anxious that their parents will not be shown the video. In a school where camcorders are often in use in classes, the help of the extra teacher in the classroom might well be enlisted to assist in videoing a class where there is a problem with pupils accepting the reality of their disruptive and silly behaviour.

There are also pupils who continuously contest the teachers' marking of their books and tests. They are the ones who feel that they are being denied recognition in the form of credits, or whatever reward systems are in place, for their work. Often their work is inadequate because they are reluctant to start until they have the promise of reward. They are aware that any improvement should be recognised but often do not understand that the standard school system cannot be devalued to give rewards on demand. Often individual teachers have given in to their demands and made it more difficult for others to resist. The support teacher can play a very useful role here in giving constant encouragement for keeping on task and negotiating with the class teacher a realistic aim for the pupil to obtain a reward. It might be that a half credit can be given on this occasion on the understanding that the other half can only be earned by similar improvement in the next lesson. Many of the children who give us the greatest cause for concern have great difficulty in persisting in a task and being consistent in this from one session to the next. In secondary schools we are patronising children and giving them an unrealistic expectation of life if we reward them for little effort, and on their own terms.

Support to build self-esteem

So many of the problems of this group of children are directly attrib-
utable to their own lack of self-esteem. Many rely on the approval of
their peers which they think can be gained by showing disregard for
the conventions of behaviour in the classroom. Unfortunately these
pupils often find that, as the rest of the class becomes more
conscious of the demands of internal and external school exams,
they are less eager to have lessons disrupted. However by this time
disruptive pupils have often become entrenched in the habit of
detecting opportunities to cause disruption. At this point they will
sometimes begin truanting rather than face the disapprobation of
their peers, or the boredom of a lesson with no light relief.

When pupils are coerced back to school after a period of truancy
there is a great need of sensitive support to make their return a
success. All too often education welfare officers work very effectively to coax pupils back into school only to see the child suspended
the next day. Often the truancy was caused by feelings of inadequacy
in the classroom, which are even more serious after a prolonged
absence. In-class or out-of-class support can play an important role
in helping these pupils to catch up with work they have missed and
listening to any problems they might be experiencing. This support
should be geared towards giving the pupil realistic feelings of
success. If the support teacher finds out that the truancy was because
of problems at home or bullying at school she is in the position to
pass this information on to those who can do something about it.

There are cases where a pupil is in the last stages of education and
it will be important to put an emphasis on the subjects where the
pupil has some hope of success. A carefully planned and supervised
period of work experience can build up self-esteem more effectively
than many school-based activities. This might be an area in which
the support teacher can help with organisation and preparation.

Support for the 'invisible' child

Most of the support we will be asked to give will be for the child
who is bringing attention to him or herself because of their noisy and
attention-seeking behaviour. There might be other children in the
classes we visit who are equally impossible to teach or to engage in
the lesson, but because they do not disrupt the education of others
they are unlikely to attract the same amount of intervention. These
are the pupils who have been described as RHINOS, or 'really here

in name only'. They are the children who are often so preoccupied with what is going on with their lives outside school that they have no mental energy left for the activities of school. Some of these are the young carers who are looking after disabled parents or helping to bring up younger children of the family. Some of them are scorned by teachers in school for their disaffection from the curriculum, but at home they are shouldering burdens and responsibilities beyond their years. Among these there might be children who are facing regular physical or sexual abuse, or mental cruelty at the hands of the people who should be caring for them.

Unless these children are in a situation where they have the confidence to disclose what is going on in their lives we are not in the position to interfere. If they should disclose serious matters to us, we should be ready to follow the guidelines that have been laid down by the local authority whilst providing sympathetic support for the child as long as the matter rests with us.

Because these children do not seek attention, they are often more difficult to engage in the curriculum than those who are eager for any type of recognition. The self-esteem of those who have received any type of abuse will be low; however those who are already shouldering the burden of caring for others might well be rewarded by the admiration of friends and neighbours and the love of younger brothers and sisters. In order to motivate 'invisible' children to complete school assignments it might be necessary to adapt material to have a far more pragmatic appeal to them. No pupils should be ignored simply because they are quiet if they are obviously not taking part in the activities of the classroom. As support teachers sitting among the pupils, we are in a unique position to make contact with pupils who are there in name only.

Summary

I consider the support of the child with emotional and behavioural difficulties the most difficult form of support to deliver in the secondary school classroom. If the problems have only become evident since transfer to high school it is relevant to look at the difference between the primary school classroom and that in the secondary school. Perhaps the most important difference is in the relationship pupils have with teachers. The classroom interactions are crucial for children whose perceptions and reactions are disturbed and whose grasp of reality might be faulty. It is important that the significant adults in their lives act in a reliable and consistent way. Any initiative which leads to all teachers co-operating in supporting any attempts to modify the children's behaviour by target setting, contracts of behaviour or sanctions must be tried. Many schools will welcome the help of the support teacher in co-ordinating this.

The child who is both disturbed and disturbing is likely to be our biggest challenge in the mainstream school. Appendix 2 describes agencies which exist to share information and support those who work with these children.

CHAPTER 6
Supporting Children with Sensory and Physical Difficulties in Mainstream Classrooms

Unless a specialist, a support teacher will support fewer children with sensory and physical difficulties than those featured in the previous three chapters. However an increasing number of these children are now coping very successfully in mainstream, and it is often easier to plan an effective programme of classroom support for them than it is for the pupils in the previous three chapters. This is not because these children's needs are in any way less special, but because there will be specially trained teachers and therapists who have been concerned with them from an early age. It would be fairly unusual for a pupil with sensory and physical difficulties to first need support on entry to secondary school, as even if the visual, hearing or physical impairment was the result of an accident, there would have been some therapeutic input from the hospital. It is very important for support teachers to have good communication with the specialist advisory teachers so that the best possible intervention can be arranged for pupils.

Of course it is absolutely possible that some of the children whose specialist support is described in this chapter might also have moderate or specific learning difficulties, or any degree of emotional or behavioural difficulty – in which case much of what is suggested in those chapters will be equally relevant for them.

The importance of liaison with specialist advisors and consultants

Most children will have had their hearing and visual problems diagnosed during their early years and their progress will have been monitored by the qualified teachers of the deaf and visually impaired. These same people might well have taught them when they were younger or have done much to support their education in their primary school. Qualified teachers in these special needs and therapists will also have made sure that any aids which they need are available and are kept in good order. The support, expertise, experience and energy of these experts is of paramount importance when a hearing or sight impaired child is integrated into any school. In primary school the liaison between the specialists and the teacher is easier as the child has just one teacher. In secondary school this is rather more difficult as any child might be taught by ten or more different teachers. In this case the SENCO will often have a regular meeting with the peripatetic teacher and then he or she will have to liaise with the staff.

It is important that the subject teachers know that expert help is available. The science or modern foreign language teachers might find it helpful to be able to talk to him or her about problems specific to their subject or even to their teaching rooms. If the peripatetic teacher cannot solve the problem fully he or she may well have contact with colleagues who have long experience of teaching sensorily impaired children in these situations and who can support the mainstream teacher who is experiencing the situation for the first time.

Children with visual difficulties in my borough are supported by a retired headteacher of a secondary school for blind children. When these children move into secondary schools, he makes it a priority to spend time with them and their teachers until the pupils have confidence in using unfamiliar equipment and moving around in new areas and the teachers have had the opportunity to learn how they can help. This initial time during the transfer from primary to secondary school is crucial. Not only will the children be in a new situation, but some teachers might also be looking after apparatus, and helping children to use apparatus, that they themselves have never used in a classroom situation before. The time that the advisor spends with the support teachers who will take on the day-to-day support is invaluable. By the time the child is settled in High School the advisor is a familiar figure in the staff room and approachable by any of the teachers or support staff.

It is important for mainstream subject teachers and support teachers to ask to be informed about any INSET on these needs that takes place in the area. A few months ago, in my borough, at the request of the support teachers, the advisory teachers for hearing and visually impaired pupils gave an after school INSET session. We all enjoyed trying the equipment and were made aware of things we might do in the classroom which could hinder our pupils. For example, we did not always realise that if we stand with our back to a window a child who is lip-reading will have greater difficulty in seeing the mouth whilst we talk, and we will disappear altogether for the child with impaired sight. When I spoke about this session with colleagues later, I encountered at least a dozen who would have attended if they had known about it.

If there is any hearing or sight impaired child in the school, all staff should know whom they should contact for advice and how to do so. It is a pity if subject teachers can only approach the advisor through someone else since the needs of the child can best be served by open communication among everyone who is responsible for his or her education.

The place of non-teaching special needs assistants

Where the child has normal learning ability, but needs help with aids, a specially trained non-teaching assistant may well be very appropriate for support in the classroom. This is particularly the case when children have congenital physical disabilities which do not interfere with their intelligence in any way. One very large comprehensive school in my area has recently taken two severely physically disabled children into Year 7. The non-teaching assistant who has aided one of the boys, a boy who has had quite severe effects of spina bifida since he was in primary school, has moved into the secondary school with him. She also looks after the needs of the other boy who has brittle bones and a growth deficiency disorder.

She accompanies both boys to their lessons as they are in the same teaching groups at present. She makes sure both are settled in the lesson; and, if there is no need for her to stay she leaves them, only returning on the rare occasions that the teacher sends for her. However, in practical lessons she is essential for holding apparatus and reaching items from shelves, etc. She has to be careful only to act on instructions from the boys and leave to them the entire decision-making process. One of the main skills she needs is to be able to do nothing until asked so that she does not make either boy more dependent on her than he need be.

The boy who needs intimate physical help is beginning to be very eager to manage more of this for himself. Breaktimes are short and it would be quicker for the assistant to do everything for him as she did in his primary school. However, part of her support function must be to support his growing independence, even though she knows that the early results might not always be perfect.

Sally, a visually impaired girl who refused to accept help from a support teacher in the classroom, was allocated a non-teaching assistant. This assistant was able to work with Sally's teachers in anticipating her needs and magnifying copies of worksheets, checking that the library could supply the large print books and talking books that were needed and being in the vicinity when Sally emerged from lessons. This was to satisfy the safety requirements of the school without interfering with Sally's desire to do it herself. Sally always made sure she had a friend with whom she could link arms, a valuable strategy which would serve her well in the outside world where support would not be allocated!

There are many experienced non-teaching assistants who are in a position to pass valuable expertise and knowledge on to those who will be providing the proposed courses to validate the training of classroom assistants. They are often the best people to support disabled children in school as, in their caring role, they can make sure that too much inappropriate pressure is not put on the integrated pupil.

For anyone who is just about to start supporting a physically handicapped youngster in school, and especially for SENCOs for whom it is a new situation, there is a very readable little book by a non-teaching classroom assistant. It describes the development of work in this field in North Wales. It is *One Step at a Time* by Margaret Slade (1990) and documents fifteen years of work as a nursery nurse supporting severely physically disabled pupils in a mainstream secondary school.

Children with hearing difficulties

The support of a child in a school where there is a unit for those with hearing difficulties is quite different from that in a school where an isolated child is being supported. This book does not intend to cover the expert support which is given by those who specialise in the education of hearing impaired young people.

A support teacher may often be asked to help a child whose intermittent hearing loss is just one item on the list of difficulties on the statement. One girl with intermediate hearing loss whom I supported, had the monotone, indistinct speech often connected with much more severe hearing loss. She had permanent grommets in both ears, but denied there was anything wrong with her hearing and stubbornly refused to sit near the front of the class. When I met her she was fourteen and had fought back against years of mockery by her classmates and, presumably the frustration of not always knowing what was going on. She always aligned herself with the high achievers in her class and copied their work. She produced beautiful neat work, but had hardly any understanding of it, and consequently always did badly in examinations. She was extremely depressed when I met her and had become very spiteful towards almost everyone in her class. Some of the girls had been patient with her dependency on them for a number of years, but now she did anything she could to annoy them. Staff were worried about her increasing alienation and her unrealistic ambition to go to university 'so she could learn to be a clever person'.

Initially she totally rejected support and said she was all right. She always suggested I go to someone else in the class who, she suggested, needed me more than she did. The girls who had always helped her were eager for her to accept support as she was hindering them. However, eventually she would make use of support if it was ostensibly given to someone else in the vicinity and she just happened to be nearby. She was unable, even in a one-to-one situation, to admit that there was anything wrong with her hearing. It was clear that she relied greatly on lip-reading and caught very little of the lesson if the teacher turned away, spoke behind her, or stood with his or her back to the window to teach.

It was decided that since she could not accept my support in the class, I should spend 45 minutes a week with her on her own. This too she tried to avoid, however, by always bringing a friend whom she said needed help. Eventually I managed, after several false starts, to engage her in a programme of Instrumental Enrichment (Feuerstein 1978) see pages 45-46. I chose this because it was unrelated to anything she had done before and therefore she would not have a fear of displaying her ignorance. We also had to talk about what we were doing so I had a chance to assess the extent of her difficulty with hearing. In the eight weeks of this support we studied two instruments. One of these comprised joining dots to form repeated shapes which were presented at a number of different angles, and the other was concerned with orientation within a space. An important element of this programme is linking what is explored in the instruments with the curriculum which is familiar to the young person. It is important also for the pupil to think about the way he or she thinks and reaches conclusions, to realise when that process is taking place and to acknowledge it with the words, 'Just a minute. Let me think!' Staff who taught her were a little bemused, until I explained, why she often said, 'ang on, I got to fink abaht it', when she was asked a question or the time came to do written work in class. However, she became much less impulsive, angry and frustrated, and, instead of tearing up work which did not reach her high expectations, completed the part of the work she was able to do well.

This girl had a behavioural difficulty which was probably the result of frustration through not always hearing what she was supposed to do. I found that she was unaware of anything I said when she was not able to see my mouth. She also probably had a learning difficulty because she was a premature baby who had passed all her milestones quite late and had spent her early years in a special diagnostic unit for vulnerable children. It was here that her hearing loss had been detected and she had thus become the responsibility of the team for hearing impaired children.

In one primary school in my borough where there is a hearing impaired unit, all the children learn to use sign language from an early age and so there is excellent integration. However, even in a situation like this hearing impaired and deaf children do suffer a great deal of frustration. In most situations this is as much to do with their indistinct speech as the distortion of the sounds they hear through their aids. Added to this is the fact that they are often the subject of bullying by other children. This bullying can be subtle and hardly detectable to the adult, who may even feel that the bully is a friend or companion. The support teacher of a hearing impaired child in a secondary school classroom will therefore have a valuable role as an advocate for the child.

Although all the staff will want to do everything possible to make life easier for the hearing impaired child, many will not realise how important it is for their mouths to be clearly visible to the child at all times. There should also be as little background noise as possible if the child is wearing an aid. It is very important for the support teacher to liaise before every lesson with the subject teacher so that it is possible to explain to the hearing impaired child exactly what he or she is expected to do. Very often such children do not have the confidence to begin a task until they see others who are on the way to completion. This is not because they are lazy and want to copy but because they often do not hear the instructions.

In many classrooms with a hearing impaired child there is a radio-link device which is worn around the teacher's neck and 'broadcasts' to the child with a hearing difficulty. A busy teacher can occasionally forget to switch this on until a crucial part of the lesson has passed, or might not check that the sound is properly adjusted. A support teacher should be alert to give the teacher a gentle reminder as often the hand of a pupil is ignored by a teacher eager to proceed with a lesson.

In one primary school in my borough where there is a hearing impaired unit, all the children learn to use sign language from an early age and so there is excellent integration. However, even in a situation like this hearing impaired and deaf children do suffer a great deal of frustration. In most situations this is as much to do with their indistinct speech as the distortion of the sounds they hear through their aids. Added to this is the fact that they are often the subject of bullying by other children. This bullying can be subtle and hardly detectable to the adult, who may even feel that the bully is a friend or companion. The support teacher of a hearing impaired child in a secondary school classroom will therefore have a valuable role as an advocate for the child.

It will also be important for teachers to make sure that there is no opportunity for bullying to take place. This is most likely to occur in the playground or in the line outside the class. However, it is possible for stealthy, carefully targeted bullying to occur within the classroom. Any child who suggests this has happened should be listened to and the situation should be investigated.

Children with visual difficulties

As explained at the beginning of this chapter, liaison with the advisory teacher and the special needs co-ordinator will be important so that both the subject and the support teacher know the nature of the child's difficulty. In some cases of visual difficulty, the child has been taught braille. In other cases there might be an appreciable amount of vision which can be maximised by using closed circuit TV, photocopying and enlarging reading matter, and experimenting with positions and angles from which to work. A child with a reduced field of vision ('tunnel vision') might, in fact, benefit from having the print size reduced so that more can be taken in. Others will benefit from having the print enlarged and will best read the blackboard from a closed circuit TV on the desk. One young man in a local grammar school finds the closed circuit TV of great value in following the experiments as well as the board work in his science lessons.

There are some visual defects which are concerned with focusing that permit the child to work with the minimum of adaptation and enlargement of materials but which entail such increased effort from the child, that without frequent breaks, he or she will become very fatigued. A young lady with nystagmus, whom I supported, was said to be able to do good work 'when she wanted to', although she was failing badly in some subjects, mainly those subjects which took place later in the day when she was suffering from intense tiredness. She was also often absent from school with headaches. However, when she was allowed to rest during the day if she felt too tired to continue, and the demands for her to produce exactly the same amount of work as her peers were waived, her attendance improved and she lost some of the impatience which was making her unpopular with staff and pupils. It was agreed that she would only be entered for those GCSE examinations in which she was likely to get above a D grade. Arrangements were made for her to sit in another room during the exams and have half-hourly breaks where she could sit back in an easy chair and rest her eyes. Some staff felt that this was not full integration! Perhaps one important role of support teachers is to explain the term 'special needs' to their colleagues. Equal access to the curriculum is precisely that. It is not synonymous with equal input or equal output.

Children with mild cerebral palsy or ataxia

These children often need little support in the classroom unless there are other learning or behavioural difficulties. They do however also become very tired because of the extra effort they need just to walk from lesson to lesson, around a large secondary school, carrying a heavy load of books with them. A support teacher sitting beside them could well add to the difficulties they already have in being seen to be different.

I have supported Derek, a young man with ataxia since he transferred from primary school to a local grammar school. He suffered oxygen deprivation shortly after birth, and the result is an uncontrollable tremor of the hands, an awkward gait and difficulty in modulating his voice and in articulating some words. At primary school, because he was unable to write legibly and his speech was underdeveloped, the level of his ability was not recognised until he won a regional chess competition. Until then he had been thought to be 'backward'. The main problem was that because his speech was slow and slurred his reading aloud was very laboured, and it was impossible to read his handwriting. Therefore, until he had access to a computer, his teachers had no idea how well constructed, creative and lively his stories were. My main role as his support teacher has been in liaising between home and school to keep the parents' expectations realistic and to help them to cope with their feelings about their son's difficulties now that they are exaggerated by the adolescent 'growth spurt'. I have also been a sympathetic ear when he has suffered periods of bullying.

The bullying Derek suffered in his first year at the grammar school was a fairly subtle, even sophisticated form of bullying. Somehow the class decided that they would elect him form captain for the second half of the second term. He was amazed and extremely flattered to be proposed and said repeatedly, 'I never knew I was so popular'. He felt that even though he did not expect to be elected he would always be pleased to have been nominated. His mother and I were surprised and not a little anxious to hear he had been unanimously elected to assume this responsibility, as the form captain read the notices every morning and was responsible for making sure the other boys waited in an orderly fashion outside the classrooms. Derek's elation was short-lived, however, as he had to repeat notices over and over again. An ostensibly helpful classmate then suggested he should *write* them on the board...an impossibility for a boy who did every bit of work on a computer. When the class misbehaved outside classrooms the pupils said it was because they did not understand what Derek wanted them to do. In this way he was forced to face all his physical weaknesses and became acutely depressed. He immediately worried that this would mean he would never be able to do.any job. Although staff soon realised what had happened and the boys were reprimanded and Derek received support during his remaining term of office, the damage was done, and for a while he felt that, not only was he useless, but he had no friends. This was the school's first experience of a physically disabled pupil and they learnt much from this painful experience. The whole process for electing form captains was discussed and reviewed.

Now eighteen months later Derek has just completed a term of duty as vice-captain, elected on his own merits, and this went well. He now feels he has a few genuine friends at the school. He is disappointed that, in terms of ability, he is in the lower half of his year group, and he has to be helped to realise that he is with the top 20 per cent of boys in his borough. There is no doubt that tiredness, and sometimes depression, hold back his academic progress. I have been able to speak to his teachers about this and about some of his difficulties with individual subjects. He uses a computer for all his writing at school and has a small bubble jet printer which enables him to print off his work without disturbing the class. It is important that any problems with his equipment are put right as soon as possible, and that he has a compatible replacement if his computer has to go away for repair.

Support teachers need to have a working knowledge of the laptop computers used by their pupils. This will be addressed in more detail in the next chapter. There is no doubt that they have made a great difference for those pupils who do not have control over their hands, and they are a great improvement over clattering typewriters.

Support for physically disabled students in the classroom will usually be to act as a pair of hands. It is important only to write what the student would have written, to work purely as a amanuensis. In these times of scarce resources, I do not consider it good use of a support teacher to sit in a laboratory or technology workshop, week after week, in order to be effective for ten or fifteen minutes of the lesson. I know of two schools where the technicians have been given extra hours so that they can support pupils. This works well as they are accustomed to the work in those departments enough to just make themselves available when needed. The other children are also used to them being there for all lessons and so it is not so obvious that they are supporting one person. One of the most stressful jobs I have done was in the school where I spent a double period each week in a chemistry laboratory to support Sue, a very able young lady with cerebral palsy. I was so bad at chemistry that I often could not understand what Sue wanted me to do. She became frustrated as she thought it was her poor articulation rather than my stupidity. In order to recompense for often failing her in her time of need, I found myself trying to be her faithful servant in other things, until one day she barked at me, 'I can do it myself. Go and help someone who can't'. Had her parents not insisted on her having the support of a qualified teacher, she would have received much more competent assistance from the lab technician who knew, from long experience, exactly what was needed and was always on hand to help. As it was her teacher had to plan practical lessons around the timetable of the support teacher.

The support Sue needed was purely technical, unlike that needed by Ella, another girl with cerebral palsy, who also has learning difficulties. Ella has had several long absences from school for major operations on her legs. Because she has become used to adult attention in hospital, she welcomes me with open arms. When I support her in science lessons it is to help her to understand processes, write her notes and read the textbook. Even without her physical disability she would probably need this kind of support. She does, however, use a laptop computer and a portable printer very effectively and is proud of her neat folders of work. Ella is a very special person to all who know her as she has such an exceptionally happy and friendly personality. She cheerfully accepts praise for the effort she puts into her work and her ambition to work in a catering situation is probably realistic.

Children in wheelchairs

It will be important for children in wheelchairs to be able to move around the school as freely as possible. This might mean teachers making sure that the layout of their rooms allows these pupils to be as independent as possible in fetching equipment for themselves. The support teachers in the classroom are in an ideal situation to give some thought to this. They can also encourage these children to use their elbow sticks if they have them as it is important for them to exercise their limbs. Indeed children with wheelchairs sometimes push their wheelchair from lesson to lesson so that their bags can be carried in it. This provides similar exercise and means they can be independent of an assistant to carry the bag.

One young man, Tim, is a pupil in a large mainstream comprehensive. He has a number of congenital physical problems and on good days can walk from lesson to lesson, but on his worst days cannot even propel his own wheelchair. There is a non-teaching assistant available at all times to assist him from lesson to lesson even if it only means carrying his 'booster' cushion. The assistant does not stay in the lesson but she can detect when he is too weary to continue on the timetable and can retire with him to a quiet room where he can have a rest or do some of the work at his own pace. Since Tim is very small it would be easy for him to be knocked over in the crush when two thousand pupils change lessons. However, pupils now know that when they see Mrs Brown, Tim must be there, and they take more care.

Integration does not mean, and cannot mean, that disabled children have to have precisely the same demands placed on them as the able bodied. Some of these children, such as those with cystic fibrosis and certain wasting diseases, have a limited life expectancy. It is important that they are able to immerse themselves in their school work for as long as possible. It must also be remembered that they are very sick children and often need support to be able to admit that they need a rest.

In a class of able bodied children hands often bob up and down when a question is asked. The disabled child might not be able to lift his or her hand that high, or keep it there, or wave it about. It is important that when the time comes for children to participate in the lesson that the wheelchair bound child does not become 'invisible'. In order to make sure that he is a full participant in the lesson, a sign that the child wishes to answer the question should be agreed at the outset.

In the playground the support of all staff at the school will be important to make sure that the child in the wheelchair is not subject to any bullying, subtle or otherwise. In this context well meaning, but patronising behaviour, may have to be gently curbed and the instigator given some explanation about why this is hurtful. It is important that other children are not allowed to make wheeling the child into a game unless it is on the specific terms of the child in the chair. It is also important for this child to be able to assert himself and be supported if he says 'No' to something which he has perhaps gone along with previously. Although some disabled children might enjoy being included in the rough and tumble of the playground, it is important for them to have the option of retiring to somewhere quieter. Ideally there should be more than one physically disabled child integrated in any one school and a quiet room should be available for them to be together when they are tired, anxious or just feel in need of mutual support.

Disabled children and bullying

As pointed out earlier in this chapter, one of the most difficult problems in the integration of children with special needs into mainstream schools has been that of bullying. Whatever projects or programmes are organised to counteract bullying, there is always a risk that it will happen. The bullies are often children who have themselves been the victims of bullies, either in school, in their neighbourhoods or in their families. It is difficult to design a programme to deter a bully who has been bullied by his or her own parents for as long as he or she can remember! In a case where the disabled child is being bullied by a child who has been the victim at other times, the problem will not be solved unless the bully also receives some kind of support in gaining insight into his or her behaviour. As illustrated in the example of Derek's experience earlier in this chapter, there is also the contagious kind of bullying where one or two of the class begin some unpleasantness, and, before those in authority are aware of what is happening, others are sucked into victimising, isolating or ridiculing a child. This can involve pupils who would otherwise not have taken part in bullying and are often full of genuine remorse when they realise how they have been influenced to behave.

It is important that the disabled child has someone to whom they can talk frankly if they suspect they are being bullied. On rare occasions the culprit could be an over-enthusiastic teacher who feels that the disabled child is taking advantage of their special status within the school. Successful support will involve sorting out the problem without alienating the disabled child from his peers or his teachers.

In writing about the support of special needs, it is important to acknowledge that these needs are so diverse that even those who have worked for many years in this field will not have come across every need. Most children have a combination of needs, and the most obvious disability might cause them less problems than a need that even those close to them are not aware exists. Children with a sensory or physical disability, who are in the final years of statutory education, are bound to have worries about their future. It might be about their careers, and there are specialist careers officers who can be contacted. However, their worries might be secret worries about their sexual development and whether their needs in this area will be fulfilled. It is important that they know someone with whom they can discuss any subject. However, well-integrated, they will need to be aware of contacts they can make with people with similar difficulties. They have had at some time the same dreams for the future as others. Sue, now in her final year at school, was told by an enthusiastic work experience co-ordinator, 'We'll have no trouble placing you. You could work as a typist now you are so good on your computer'. She retorted, 'Yes, but I'd really like to be an air hostess'. As well as being an extremely efficient typist she is gifted in modern foreign languages and loves to fly abroad with her family every year. Without cerebral palsy she would be well qualified to achieve her ambition. Efforts are being made for her to obtain a work experience with an airline as ground staff at the airport, for this an airline is willing to make a two week commitment and 'see how it goes'. If she could eventually be considered for this kind of employment she might wear the uniform and benefit from discounted travel later. However it will, like so many of the careers these young people hope for, be second best!

There are some useful addresses in Appendix 2 for those teaching the hearing impaired and the visually handicapped.

CHAPTER 7
The use of computers and audio equipment in classroom support

The fact that Professor Stephen Hawkin is known throughout the world as a best selling author of a scientific treatise and a compelling lecturer is evidence of the change that computer technology has made to the lives and careers of severely disabled people. Without tailor-made technology to help him, this man would be unable to speak or write and might even be referred to sorrowfully as a 'vegetable'. There are many less dramatic cases of disability where the support of information technology has opened up education to young people. There are still more young people who, whilst not being dependent on computers, are empowered and motivated by their use.

This chapter will add to the strategies referred to in the previous five chapters, and some uses of computers and audio equipment may be repeated. This is because many strategies designed for one sort of difficulty are adaptable and easily transferable to another. In a single chapter it is not possible to give a comprehensive account of the many ways in which information technology can be used to support the work in secondary school classrooms. An informative and interesting book on this subject is *Learning Difficulties and Computers: Access to the Curriculum* (Hawkridge and Vincent 1992). In this there are case studies of successful and empowering use of computers both in this country and in the USA.

The need for INSET in IT for support teachers

Perhaps one of the greatest INSET needs at present in SEN is for teachers to understand the use of information technology in the classroom. Children are being issued with laptop computers of which they have high hopes. Many really believe that once their laptop arrives all their problems with illegible and painfully executed writing, bad spelling and untidy layout will disappear as if by some kind of magic.

A thirteen-year-old boy, Jeremy, knew that the provision of a laptop computer was written into his statement of SEN. His progress had been held back all through his school life by his severe specific learning difficulties. He had a great store of knowledge and stories in his head, but found it almost impossible to produce anything intelligible on paper. It was evident how able he was during the short period when a support teacher scribed for him. The computer arrived the day before the Easter vacation. It was handed to him in a box with a carrying case and a large manual. 'All you need to know is in there', he was told, 'take it home and you will know all about it by next term'. Staff were annoyed when Jeremy 'forgot' to bring the computer back the following term. When he had failed to bring it for the whole of the first week, his support teacher was asked to make a home visit to find out what had happened to it. It was quite safe, in the box and hardly used. Jeremy certainly could not begin to read the manual, and the parents were embarrassed about the difficulty they had understanding what it meant although they could technically read it.

Jeremy had had six years of failure in school. He certainly was not going to risk failing again, even though he had this 'magic' aid which he knew was the envy of his class. Fortunately a PGCE student from a local college was doing a study on the use of IT in SEN and had offered to help individual children to understand their computers. This student, Heather, spent some valuable time with Jeremy, familiarising him with the functions of the laptop and building his confidence. Thanks to her help, he was soon able to move text around the small screen, use the spell checker and print out his work. I think that had it not been possible to enlist this extra help, the computer would have been returned unused and Jeremy would have felt that he had to cope with yet another failure.

We were fortunate that during the term that this student was attached to the department, she were able to give initial support to more than a dozen pupils who were using personal laptops for the first time. She generously gave her telephone number to a disabled boy whose needs would change with the curriculum, and I know that he has found her ongoing support invaluable. Perhaps when support staff are recruited we should put more emphasis on their ability to give this specific kind of help to pupils. They require enough basic knowledge of information technology to be able to interpret the various, often badly written, manuals which come with the computers, and with some of the software. They need just enough knowledge of programming to understand how to input information into an existing programme in order to fit it to the needs of an individual pupil, and they need to know where to find out this information and anything else that crops up.

Because Heather was a student she had time to work individually with pupils in the initial stages so that they could give their whole attention to the task in hand. Often this was done before or after school, or during break so that pupils did not fall further behind, but much was done during the day. On a number of occasions she attended every lesson during the first day that a pupil was using a laptop computer in class. Often this event can cause disruption as other pupils want to 'have a go'. This causes teachers much anxiety as they fear that in this situation there could be accidents. Heather was able to supervise other children's attempts and lay down some ground rules for the future. If support teachers are to do this work, then they will have to have a flexible timetable and be released from other duties for a time.

In one school, where many of the sixth form are working for qualifications in IT, a sixth former is paired with any special needs pupil who has a computer. The sixth formers can spend time helping the younger children to maximise the use of the technology, and at the same time widen their own knowledge of the use of computers. Some may feel that there is a narrow margin between enlisting the help of sixth formers to help with younger pupils on tasks that will, in fact, help the older student to develop skills and knowledge, and using sixth formers in the place of staff whose salaries would place an unacceptable strain on the school budget. It is important when enlisting the help of students that the exercise is of mutual benefit.

Supporting learning difficulties

There is plenty of documented evidence about the benefit of using educational programmes on the computer with children with both severe and moderate learning difficulties. There are a number of excellent special programmes which break concepts down into easily manageable stages and keep the user on an appropriate stage with a variety of examples at that level until the element is grasped. It is unlikely that a support teacher in a secondary school classroom will have to work with children who are so severely disabled that they need help with achieving even a single movement and have to be helped to build up to a useful sequence of movements. However, many will work with pupils with a very poor sight vocabulary, and some pupils with learning difficulties will need extra support from the teacher before they can confidently use the programme being used by the rest of the class. It will be important that the support teacher is familiar with the programme and is in a position either to teach some of the vocabulary first or to provide easily understood prompt cards.

When supporting Hazel, a girl with almost no memorised vocabulary in a French lesson, a support teacher provided all the vocabulary for a game on cards with the words and actions depicted beside them. By the end of the game, Hazel had learnt two of the words and could identify them without looking at the cards.

Many computer programmes can be personalised with the individual school's and pupil's details. It is very useful for the support teacher to know how to input the necessary details so that the pupil is not faced with initial failure. I am not attempting to list computer programmes here since there are constant additions to existing resources and updating of hardware. It is very important for those supporting special needs to be aware of what is available. At the end of this chapter there is a section on keeping up to date with new developments in educational information technology.

The language development of pupils with special needs can also be helped by using tape recorders. Children with overall poor ability often derive tremendous pleasure from hearing themselves on tape, especially if they have helped with the planning and editing of the tape and what they have said is well rehearsed so that they can feel proud to keep the tape as evidence of success. If a magazine programme is to be made pupils often have a chance to share with peers their enthusiasm and expertise about hobbies which are not familiar to the others. A support teacher decided to complete a term's withdrawal work with a small group of Year 7 pupils by making a magazine programme that they could play to the rest of the class. No one knew that Lenny was an expert on garden pools. He started talking about the problems of reaching the right balance of chemicals to keep the water pure enough for the fish but to provide nutrients for the plants. He also quoted examples of how careless use of some substances could erode the sides and bottom of the pond. It was decided that Robert would interview him about this. Lenny, who could hardly read and who produced pages and pages of illegible, unintelligible writing, sounded every inch the learned scientist on the 'programme'. The other children in the class could not believe it was him. His father's family were Romanies who specialised in landscape gardening, and he listed the large properties in the area that they had enhanced with the addition of a decorative pond.

Tape recorders are particularly valuable in work with pupils with specific learning difficulties. Michelle was in Year 10 and very embarrassed about her inability to complete a piece of creative writing. Her head was full of good stories and when she had the opportunity to dictate them to a scribe she managed to keep a number of characters in play and maintain the tension to the end. However, if she was working by herself, she continually went back over the first couple of sentences to remember what she had written. Often the spelling was so bizarre that she could not understand it anyway. Before long she would be looking at her watch to see how long the lesson would last, complaining of a headache, or asking to go to the lavatory. It was suggested that she should record her stories during the lesson and check them through to make sure that she had recorded what she wanted to. She was provided with an Amstrad NC100 computer with rechargeable batteries. This machine weighs less than a kilo and is only the size of a piece of A4 paper, so she could slip this easily into her bag to take home. At home she had to listen to the tape, sentence by sentence, on her Walkman. She had to write down each sentence and use the spell checker as she went along. She handed in the computer to her support teacher who further checked the spelling and discussed any doubtful sentences with Michelle. Michelle would then go to the learning resource centre at lunch-time and print out her work, ready to give in. She did not mind the extra time it took her as she said that she felt like a real secretary as she sat typing at the dressing table in the bed and break-fast hostel where she and her mother had temporary accommodation. At a very difficult time in her life this girl received a tremendous boost from having the means to produce her work independently. An important spin-off has been that her word processing skills are so good that she should have little difficulty in finding employment later.

Many of the pupils who have statements because of their specific learning difficulty have been issued with these personal laptop computers and, if given satisfactory initial help, find them invaluable. But this is not the only way in which IT is used by these pupils. There is much software designed specifically for those with sequencing difficulties and problems with reading and spelling. It would be impossible to list all the companies and sources here, but journals produced by the National Association for Special Educational Needs (NASEN) and by the British Dyslexia Association run regular reviews of programmes which have been found to be effective. Since it is difficult for an individual teacher to try out every programme, reviews written by practising teachers are an invaluable source of information and are not to be confused with the descriptions given by the producers of the software. Just because the software is produced by a trained teacher, it will not necessarily be geared effectively to special needs.

It is important to find out if there are IT experts in other schools and if a special needs IT group exists in your area. Many of the special schools have formed a group to meet regularly and exchange information. They often have licences to copy some of the more expensive specialist programmes. They are usually pleased to welcome any teachers from mainstream schools who have an interest in serving the needs of these children. If there is no such group, perhaps you could suggest that one is formed in your area as often individual schools are reluctant to buy a licence for a programme which is not of universal use.

Supporting emotional and behavioural difficulties

It is the children with emotional and behavioural difficulties (EBD) who often cause the most concern to teachers as they cannot be ignored. However these same children who can make the lives of other teachers so difficult can often be found in their IT lessons, quietly and totally absorbed in their work. Recently I was asked to do supply cover for a class of boys I knew very well. I was told they were in the computer room. To my surprise the two boys who were notorious for disrupting classes in the school did not even look up when I entered. In fact these boys had been working without any teacher in the room for the last ten minutes.

Children with EBD usually have a problem with concentrating but because they are controlling the actions of the computer they are able to sustain their efforts. The physical position of the child at the keyboard is such that he is virtually cut off from his neighbours whilst looking at the screen. There is also the fear that if he leaves his work station someone else might come in and claim it. Watching these disruptive pupils working with IT demonstrates how much of their potential is wasted with the distractions of the classroom.

These children often do not have the concentration to work on the really small notepad computers which have only a narrow screen, but they will produce excellent work if they can be given the opportunity to use a desktop machine. Those who are used to teaching these pupils will be familiar with the frustration of trying to obtain a piece of work from children who are so critical of their attempts that they repeatedly tear up the paper when they have only done the first few lines because of one spelling mistake. Once they master word processing they reach a new level of expression as they can constantly go back and correct on-screen before committing themselves to a printed copy. In this situation a facility to enable the pupil to have a preview of the printed page on-screen is almost essential. They can then adjust the layout of their work before exposing it to anyone else. The production of neat work by means of the word processor is very important in building up the self-esteem of these pupils and can have a knock-on effect as they have less need of their own work-avoidance strategies to disturb the work of others, or to put on a performance in their role as class-clown.

It is well worthwhile for a support teacher to find out how time in the computer room or learning resource base in a school is allocated. It could be that there are regular times during the week when it is not in use, or is used by small sixth form groups and there are some free workstations. If this is so, it might be possible to take very small groups of special needs children there to perform specific tasks. Indeed, if they are sharing the room with another group, this can be a positive benefit as they will have to be considerate to the group and will have the opportunity to see other uses of the technology; it could also well be that an older student can give them advice on layout, and other special functions of the computer about which the special needs teacher has no knowledge.

Many EBD pupils also have moderate or specific learning difficulties. Needless to state, strategies mentioned in the section on learning difficulties are as relevant to the EBD children as they are to the sensorily and physically impaired children who have learning difficulties.

Supporting hearing, visually and physically impaired pupils and students

This is such a huge area with ever-improving technology available that it is not possible to cover all possibilities in a complete book, let alone part of one chapter. It is important that support teachers have easy access to up-to-date information. The main support group for those who are concerned with the education of children with special educational needs is the National Association for Special Educational Needs. Members of this Association have formed an IT Interest Group. This group intends also to hold in-service training for teachers, both those who are nervous of technology and those who have experience which they wish to increase. The address for NASEN is: NASEN, York House, Exhall Grange, Wheelwright Lane, Coventry CV7 9HP. Among these pupils there will be those who are totally reliant on technology in order to reach their full potential and there will be those for whom it is merely a welcome aid to make their lives a little easier.

For pupils with little or no sight, taped texts of all kinds are essential. There are many texts available from the: Audio Reading Trust, The RNIB, 224 Great Portland Street, London W1N 6AA. However, teachers who support visually impaired pupils in the mainstream will find it useful to obtain worksheets and short texts that are going to be used during the term so that they can record these on to a tape. This way the pupil does not have to rush to complete work whilst the support teacher is available to read it aloud.

It can be very helpful to gradually compile a revision tape, with the main aspects of each lesson on it, during the term. This can be used as a checklist by the pupil and if gaps are left at regular intervals pupils can insert their own information.

If the school has access to a printer that can transform the written word into braille, the support teacher can anticipate the needs of the pupil for revision notes, etc. This machine will be even more useful if the pupils themselves have sufficiently accurate keyboard skills to type in their own notes. They can then be printed out for the teacher to check before being turned into braille for the student to study.

If you are supporting a pupil with any of these needs it will be important to discuss the use of information technology with specialist teachers and advisors.

Keeping up-to-date

Since there are constant developments in this field it is important to regularly read a publication which reports on this. The *Times Educational Supplement* has a section devoted to IT every Friday, and regularly runs a special pull-out feature on this. A visit to the annual Special Needs Exhibition presented by NASEN is an opportunity to see software in action. It is also worth asking to be added to the mailing list of the National Council of Educational Technology (NCET), since they produce frequent publications with up-to-date information about developments in educational IT. The Association for Computers in Education (ACE), and Computability, are other organisations which give specialist help and advice in using IT to support children with special needs. Information on all these organisations is available from NCET.

It is also useful to belong to a local user group so that resources can be shared and difficulties discussed. Even those teachers who have studied information technology as part of their initial training will need to regularly make sure that they can use new programmes and even new machines.

CHAPTER 8

Effective support and the Code of Practice

What is effective support?

There are mixed feelings about the changes that have taken place in Education in the last decade. Initiatives which have put educational services on a market place footing have been of particular concern to those concerned with special educational needs. As central services have been dismantled and reformed as private agencies, the concept of effectiveness, or 'value for money', has become more and more important.

When the opportunity for a research project was presented to me whilst I was working as a peripatetic support teacher it was these considerations which led me to try to undertake a study on the effectiveness of classroom support. It seemed obvious that, as more and more peripatetic teams became self-financing agencies, and more and more individual special needs teachers were working independently, it would be important to ensure that classroom support was giving value for money. I therefore set myself the task of finding a set of indicators of effective classroom support.

Plan of research

The study (Lovey 1993) involved eight secondary schools in an outer London Borough (five LEA and three grant-maintained, one of which was a grammar school), and consisted of a series of semi-structured interviews with headteachers, SENCOs, subject and support staff, the children being supported and their parents. Similar questions were put to each interviewee. A range of issues were explored, especially the following:

- whether support was more effective in-class or by withdrawal;
- whether secondary pupils are embarrassed by in-class support;

- whether support is more effective in some subjects than others;
- how personality and personal philosophy affects the interaction between the subject and support teacher;
- how effective support can be defined;
- how the contents of the statements of SEN affect the quality of support.

What now follows is a summary of the main findings which emerged through discussion of each of these issues and the conclusions I drew regarding the key factors in effective support.

Withdrawal or in-class support?

Teachers, SENCOs and headteachers were keen to engage in discussions about the value of in-class versus withdrawal support. Opinions were wide ranging. At one extreme, this is what one headteacher said of in-class support:

> Absolute rubbish – first class balderdash and the worse kind of rhetoric. Most kids respond to attention, praise, parameters in which to work. They can't work when they feel embarrassed. Sometimes they cannot work with the support teacher because the chemistry is wrong. Teachers say this because they are expected to say it.

In contrast, another headteacher admitted that on the whole staff preferred in-class support, while acknowledging that there is still the odd call for a 'sin-bin'. There were two schools where there was no withdrawal support at all. The teacher in one of the schools said:

> Opinion is divided. It is politically correct to prefer in-class support.

Whereas the teacher from a school where there was no firm policy on one kind of support or the other stated quite clearly:

> Personally I like in-class support. It's good. With withdrawal support I don't know what is going on; neither does the child who is being taken out. I find it better to keep it all as a great big unit.

Both these teachers had trained in the early 1960s and had spent over twenty years teaching their own subject in mainstream schools. One headteacher, who had come to the post fairly recently said:

> I don't know if I agree. Most people here accept it because it is school policy, not necessarily because it is the best way of doing

things.

Although the support teachers all gave examples of effective work that they had done with individual children on a one-to-one basis, for all except one this was the exception rather than the rule. The one who was expected to withdraw children from lessons had this comment to make:

It's always a problem if you use a free room for individual support because when you get there you often find someone else is using it. Sometimes they come in just as you have started work and you have to find somewhere else.

It was clear that parents needed some reassurance about the aims of in-class support as comments from mothers were:

If he's got 0.1 on his statement it is easier to know if he actually gets this if you know when he gets the extra time. You can ask him when he gets home what he has learnt. If it's just vague help by a teacher in the classroom she might be helping another child during your time.

Another mother found it equally difficult to understand the role of the support teacher in-class:

It (the statement) says he needs help with reading and writing. He says a lady comes into Science and does it for him. I don't think that helps him to do it himself. I don't want him to miss Science. I think he should have his extra in English time.

Another mother had very understandable concerns about conducting a lesson within a lesson:

I think it must be difficult to try to teach something different to a child in the classroom where a lesson is going on. It must be difficult for the child to know who to listen to.

One mother was apologetic about her concerns for her son who had been withdrawn for help in the primary school:

He really enjoys his lessons at the big school and he likes being helped by the support lady. He says that she's not there just for him and A (another statemented child) but she helps anyone who wants help. I worry that he doesn't get enough help if others who don't need it are being helped. I would like him to have real reading lessons.

Reading was also the concern of the mother of a school leaver:

I am glad she is going to have her examinations read to her but I don't understand why the extra help she had didn't take her to a quiet place and teach her to read.

However one parent who had been unhappy at school because she was in the 'soft kids' group', said:

We only met the others at P.E. and games. I was good at games but the kids from the hut never got chose for the team. I'd rather our *E* enjoyed his school and had friends and got picked for football, even if he is still behind. At least he can have help in class.

This boy was at the school where the head was the most scathing about in-class support!

Overall the headteachers were more certain about the value of in-class support than the SENCOs or the subject teachers. The headteachers were also much more inclined to say that withdrawal from class puts pupils at a disadvantage.

Do secondary school pupils find in-class support embarrassing?

Unlike the mothers, most of the SENCOs were anxious that no child should be seen to be the target of the support teacher's attention. The SENCO at a school where the headteacher insisted that there be no withdrawal said:

I think most pupils prefer not to be supported as individuals. The best way to conceal that support is through working in the classroom. I think that if you take a youngster out of the classroom, then obviously they are identified. If you support an individual in the class they are identified and they know it. Most prefer in-class support not directed to them.

This was the school where the mother wanted to be really sure her son actually received the 0.1 support specified on his statement! The SENCO in another school that provides both in-class and withdrawal support said:

You have to realise secondary pupils do prefer support as long as it is subtle. We have to be quite subtle in the way support takes place. The support always has to be such that you don't single out individuals clearly within the room.

If the SENCOs were cautious about individual children receiving support conspicuously, what did the pupils themselves think? One pupil (quoted on the subject in Chapter 3, p.41) was adamant about the importance of having support in the classroom that was targeted to the child who needed it, quite a different position from that of the SENCO.

A Year 7 boy, when asked if he found in-class support embarrassing, seemed absolutely baffled by the question:

> I would feel embarrassed if I suddenly found I was in the wrong room with a different class. I would be embarrassed if I was in a class with all girls. I don't think anything else is embarrassing especially, but there might be.

Although well over half of the professionals were concerned that the adolescent pupil would find targeted in-class support embarrassing not one of the pupils stated that this was so. One boy, however, said that he preferred the others to think that the support teacher helped him because she liked him.

Is support more effective in some subjects than others?

Some interviewees immediately agreed with this question, but then on reflection decided that the effectiveness of support often depended less on the subject content and more on the compatibility of the personalities of the class-teacher and the support teacher. Two of the headteachers also expressed this view. One said:

> Subject support does not matter – it is the nature of the interaction process that is important.

And the other, with greater emphasis:

> No. I don't think the subject has anything to do with it at all. It is the nature of the interaction that is concerned. The question is an insult to teachers. It does not matter what you are teaching, it is a process. If you are subject dependent you have vast problems.

However, the headteacher of the only selective school in the sample was concerned about teachers supporting subjects with which they were not familiar. He said:

> We could do with more support in science but most support teachers are primary trained and could not do it.

Overall the SENCOs were more likely than the headteachers to differentiate between the subjects when evaluating the work of support teachers. The SENCO of one school held the view that non-specialist support could be a positive advantage:

> ...sometimes it is better not to know more about the subject...and then you have some idea of the difficulties that the student is experiencing and you can ask the teacher for clarification.

This one recognised that some teachers were more sympathetic to support than others:

> There might be some subjects where the support viewpoint is better received. Here support in modern languages is good but in that department we have people who really welcome support.

One of the SENCOs also had misgivings about Science, although she was enthusiastic about support in other subjects:

> I think it can be very effective in Maths and English and some of the humanities. I have found it very difficult in Science. I should think it is easier if you are a scientist yourself but it is very difficult to know what the pupils are doing before you go into class.

Similar enthusiasm about support in English and the humanities was expressed by another SENCO:

> If you are talking about a subject like English or the humanities, it is almost entirely language-based – then it's going to be much more applicable than in a technology lesson.

And again the humanities are mentioned by another SENCO:

> ...geography where a lot of different skills are needed and children need a lot of help with that. Materials need differentiating, especially in subjects such as history. The vocabulary is very difficult and, depending on the reason for the statement, support in science, writing notes, can be very useful. In French very much depends on how much group work is done and how much class teaching.

The opinions of the teachers were similar to those of the SENCOs, agreeing that support was more effective is some subjects than others. In the school where the headteacher had been scornful of the suggestion that some subjects might be more effectively supported than others, one teacher said:

> It would be more helpful in some lessons than others. On the literacy side you need some help. It may well be that you are doing something where you need to read instructions...Some children are in danger in a practical lesson if they don't have some

kind of support. It would take them out of the curriculum area if they didn't have support in science and CDT. I have heard a criticism from the Science Department that the child would be a danger.

And another commented:

I think it would be more effective in subjects with complicated vocabulary and heavy reading. I think it would be useful in geography, history, science...you might need support in a mixed ability class for GCSE English. The more technical subjects need support.

When parents were asked about which subjects lent themselves best to support, they, like the headteachers and unlike the SENCOs, tended to put emphasis on the teacher's personality rather than the subject. As one mother said:

R likes to have support in science. Last year the teacher didn't like him so he asked his support teacher for help. This year he likes Mr X and he helps him to do his work so he doesn't bother with the support teacher.

And similarly another mother said:

I wish someone would go into E's lesson with Mr Y. I don't think Mr Y likes E. I know E doesn't like Mr Y. He says he doesn't understand him and he won't explain the work properly to him so I think they should get a support teacher to go in there with him. He did have trouble with his French teacher but I think that has changed now.

Pupils too put emphasis on personality. One pupil was quite clear that the teacher made more difference than the subject:

The subject does not make a difference, but the teacher does. If there is a teacher where we muck around in the lesson it's better if I have a support teacher. If I do I mess around, because I am big I get caught...Yes, sometimes I don't know how to stop, especially if I am near D, or people are laughing.

How does personality and personal philosophy affect the interaction between the subject teacher and the support teacher?

The personalities and philosophies of the class-teacher and the support teacher, and the way in which they interacted, was a recurring theme throughout the interviews with the professionals. There was an attempt to focus mostly on the personal issues surrounding support. There were teachers who were eager that others should not find out that they were not happy about having a support teacher in the classroom as they felt they would be criticised for their attitude. These teachers nearly always then mentioned the name of a teacher who was an exception to this, and whom they would welcome because of their personality.

The importance of compatibility was stated very strongly by head-teachers:

Sometimes they cannot work with a support teacher because the chemistry is wrong.

And:

Not a simple question – combination of factors – often it is a matter of personalities.

And:

Depends on the teacher – personality and philosophy – rather than the subject.

Yet another headteacher agreed with the importance of the interaction in the classroom team:

Nothing to do with the subject but the relationship between the support teacher and the teacher.

SENCOs also placed importance on the teachers' personalities rather than the subjects:

Depends on the nature of the person, not the subject.

One specifically mentioned methods and philosophy:

It depends on the methods, the philosophy and the personality of the teacher. Some teachers are not amenable to any change in their method of teaching...Some teachers here have been resentful of support in the classroom.

Another SENCO expressed concern about this aspect of support:

It depends on the personality of both teachers...I don't think there's any prescription for how they work. It seems they work better when the teachers get on – as people. They don't have to be best buddies, but where they like each other as people. Where there is hostility or antipathy it is an enormous problem for support teachers and I don't know how to get around it.

A colleague was more optimistic:

> When I came here there were some people who gave support, but some were hostile at first. Now they gladly accept support in their classrooms. One of them has been at the school 35 years and was very against it, but now accepts it.

Overall, there was strong support among the headteachers, SENCOs and teachers that some subject teachers find the presence of a support teacher very uncomfortable or threatening and that some teachers would prefer to have help so that they could support their own pupils with SEN directly.

How can we define effective support?

This question was included as a response to the concern expressed in the Audit Commission's report (1992) that support was not being targeted to the need written into the statement and the fact that there seemed to be little attempt to monitor support. Although nearly all respondents mentioned testing, reviewing and discussing progress with those concerned, there was difficulty in defining an effective support strategy. As one headteacher explained:

> It is too complex an issue for you to have objective criteria where you might see how a child has progressed through formal tests, in-class tests or other procedures. You might find it associated with behavioural situations so that if you solve the behaviour, the child improves and the children round him get a fair crack of the whip. Sometimes it is used as a holding provision – the criteria given is that less children are excluded...It could be that the member of staff is not sufficiently skilled and they need the support teacher more than the child...Statement support is a counter-productive use of resources. The only way it can be evaluated is if the dynamics of the classroom change so that the other children gain because the teacher has more time.

He was unconvinced that individual statements served any purpose and would only see a strategy that benefited all pupils as effective.

A reliable gauge of the value-added factor was seen by some to be important:

> I suppose you have to know where the child was at the beginning of the support. You need to test the child before and after to

measure the effectiveness...you have to find some way of measuring it and I don't think it is that difficult.

The SENCO at this school saw the support teacher as the one who should monitor the effectiveness of the intervention:

It is important for the support teacher to specify precisely where the improvement has been made.

And a teacher at the same school suggested:

It would be nice if we had a report on every lesson.

In one school, where the headteacher favoured testing at preset intervals, the SENCO said:

I do not think there is any clear-cut way of saying it is very good, or it is very bad. I don't think it is something we can do in ticked boxes. It's incredibly difficult. I think every subject is different and the support teacher can work in a variety of ways and I am not sure you can analyse that with just a set of boxes. The children we withdraw on the literacy programme are regularly reading tested or spelling tested and all children are tested before they have an annual review so you've got scores there.

The SENCO of another school had similar reservations:

We have to be careful not to evaluate purely on the kind of form this government likes, with tick boxes and the like, because, for instance...the level of language might not be better but the attitude might be better. He might be more willing to learn.

The professionals did not see any reliable assessment as easily achievable as they distrusted their own skills in testing literacy; they spoke of reviewing or evaluating the progress a child had made on the basis of some objective data:

This I feel to be difficult. I have been trained non-academically to be very wary of raw scores, and reading exams and that kind of thing, but I realise that if we are not careful we are very much into the 'I think he appears to have improved' phrases with very little broad data to support it.

One SENCO suggested that testing pupils would be very difficult as there are long periods when a child does not appear to be progressing:

I think that kind of crude way of evaluating children's learning is not particularly valuable because children don't learn to order, do they? I mean...you look back after six months and see how much progress a child has made and you can't detect the progress. I don't think that means the support has not been effective whereas the equation would suggest that, so I don't think it is overuseful, although it is one way...I wouldn't use standardised tests at the beginning and the end, but that does not mean I would rule that out as something that would be useful.

Parents were clearly in favour of testing:

They should give him a reading test, a spelling test and a maths test every term and tell us the results.

And:

I would like to have some idea of if he is getting better. Perhaps if they gave him a test every term we could look and see if he was getting any better and if the help was worth it.

Another parent suggested an effective way of evaluating support would be to ask the parents of the supported children what they thought:

Independent reports from parents? I think if people spoke to me I could give them some idea, although I am not *au fait* with everything that goes on at school...I could sit down and talk about certain periods in *R's* life and say how he benefited and why...if you are going to ask individual teachers, they are all going to have a different viewpoint anyway, aren't they, depending on the lessons? The tutors would be the people to go to. I think someone like *F.O.* (the form tutor) who has taken an interest in *R's* overall education.

Another parent expressed a concern to have a more regular update on his son's progress:

I suppose the only way you can see if the money is making any difference is to wait for the regular review. Perhaps someone should come to us every quarter and have a general chat to see how things are going.

One of the headteachers was in favour of talking not only to the parents but to everyone concerned with the child:

You can talk to the teacher in whose class the child is receiving support; you can talk to the pupil; you can talk to the parents and talk to the support teacher.

The need for well written statements of special need

Inextricably linked with the problem of evaluating support was the consideration of the original needs listed on the statement. This headteacher was not the only professional who commented on the use of the term 'differentiated curriculum':

> If statements are clearly written and the needs of the child properly described it would be (possible to evaluate support) yes you could then attach success criteria to it. But I find that many of the statements, when they come back, are not clear, then you have to spend some time unpacking what it is, and then you are still not clear that you have unpacked it correctly. Therefore, when it comes round for review you're still not sure that you have achieved, what you should have done, as you're still not sure what it was. For example, 'the child needs access to a differentiated curriculum', but differentiated by what? by task? by outcome? what does that mean? How do we know it has been differentiated? The system is open to abuse.

Another headteacher said:

> The statements are often not about what is written on them. If you look a little deeper they are about difficulties teachers have with certain children.

One headteacher was suspicious of the role of the new statementing officer appointed in the borough:

> I wonder if this is part of the role of the new officer...if that is to account for whether it provides an improved quality of learning, or whether it is a means of accounting for the money, whether it is merely an administrative post. I am just not too sure about that role but wondered if it was just to respond to the Audit Commission's report by putting it on paper to explain how the money has been spent, rather than approach any form of evaluation how effective, how it's improved learning experience, or how it has benefited the child...

Twelve key factors of effectiveness in statement support

Although there were many differences of opinion with regard to many issues, during the course of interviewing headteachers,

SENCOs, teachers, parents and children a number of factors were elicited which seemed to point to effective support. These can be stated as follows:

(1) The personal involvement of the senior management team with the delivery of support, and high status given to the post of SENCO.

(2) Good communication between all those concerned with the statemented child.

(3) Time allocated for liaison between all the child's teachers and parents.

(4) Recognition of the link between learning difficulties and behavioural difficulties, and the building of self-esteem.

(5) A positive personality and philosophy on the part of the support teacher.

(6) Compatibility between the subject and support teacher.

(7) The appointment of a special needs co-ordinator for each faculty or subject area.

(8) Availability of material resources for support.

(9) Availability of specialist advice for Special Educational Needs.

(10) INSET provision.

(11) The facility for withdrawal for a specific purpose, even when the general policy was for in-class support.

(12) Covert delivery of support for some secondary school pupils, depending on the pupil's temperament.

Some of the problems mentioned in this chapter have been addressed in the Code of Practice for the Identification and Assessment of Special Educational Needs (DfE 1994). However it is still important, not only for the statemented pupils involved, but also for the sake of the professionalism of the emerging category of the support teacher, that the delivery of effective support is recognised as a skill with its own special value, part of which is making children with special needs feel valued.

Support and the Code of Practice

At the time when I was undertaking my research and discussing support with teachers, parents and pupils, concern was often expressed about the inconsistency of provision and the criteria by which it was accessed. There was difficulty in deciding how the effectiveness of the use of the resources could be monitored, and how successful practice would be measured. We now have a Code of

Practice on the Identification and Assessment of Special Educational Needs which, in the first paragraph states its purpose:

...to give practical guidance to LEAs and the governing bodies of all maintained schools – and to all those who help them, including health services and social services – on the discharge of their services under Part III of the Education Act 1993.

A summary of the stages was given in Chapter 1, and further details can be found in Appendix 1. It is important that all those who are concerned with special education, in any way, have access to a copy of this Code. All teachers would benefit from INSET training on the contents and aims of the document that is already known, by its abbreviated title, as 'The Code of Practice'.

In the preceding section, I have suggested twelve key indicators of effective statement support. It now seems appropriate to see to what extent the Code of Practice would make these factors easier to achieve.

The involvement of the senior management team in special needs provision, and the status of the SENCO

It is made clear from the Code that the senior management team must be involved in all stages, and not merely at the stage where it has been decided to apply for a statement. The suggestion that, in a small school, the headteacher or deputy should take on the duties of the SENCO is an interesting one. Of course, if time was allowed for this person to fulfil all the responsibilities comprising the SENCO's job, he or she would have difficulty in undertaking much other administrative work. However, this would at least give special needs high status within the school, and therefore the advice and training would be taken more seriously by the staff.

It is clear, by the list of duties, that the post of SENCO, will be a pivotal one within any school which has a comprehensive or non-selective intake of pupils. The specific responsibilities are laid down as follows:

– the day-to-day operation of the school's SEN policy
– liaising with and advising fellow teachers
– co-ordinating provision for children with special educational needs
– maintaining the school's SEN register and overseeing the records on all pupils with special educational needs

- liaising with parents of children with special educational needs
- contributing to the in-service training of staff
- liaising with other external agencies including the educational psychology service and other support agencies, medical and social services and voluntary bodies. (pp.9–10)

It is acknowledged, in the same section, that large schools might well need a learning support team led by the SENCO.

The fact that all mainstream schools will have to publish a special needs policy with details of their arrangements, staffing, in-service training, outside links and the specialist qualifications of staff should raise the status of the whole department throughout the school community.

Good communication between all those concerned with the statemented child

All the stages in the Code of the identification and assessment process entail all the professionals who are concerned with the child meeting together. Although there is no obligation for the parents to come into the school for a meeting during the first stage, they must be informed that this stage has been initiated. After the meeting to discuss the needs of the child at this stage the parents must be informed of the outcome and the strategies that are being used to help their child. The parents whom I met all expressed concern that they did not know that there was any difficulty until it was really serious. Once the Code is implemented this process can be triggered by concern expressed early on by one of the child's teachers, the child's parents, a social worker or a health professional.

It is important that as well as collecting information from teachers and parents and using information already available from the social and health services, the children themselves are also to be consulted about how they perceive the difficulties.

If further stages are implemented this information will simply be updated or added to. In the school-based Stages 2 and 3, the professionals involved meet together for reviews and to draw up an Individual Educational Plan (IEP). The difference between Stages 2 and 3 is that at Stage 3 a special needs support team is brought in to help with planning for the pupil; and at this stage there is an expectation that parents will actually be present at the planning meeting. However parents are entitled to attend a meeting earlier than this, and must be informed of what is happening at each and every stage, instead of only knowing there are difficulties when the child reaches Stage 4, as has often been the case.

It will not be possible to draw up an IEP in a secondary school without all the staff concerned communicating with each other and the SENCO. One of the main tasks of the SENCO will be concerned with making sure that this level of communication is made possible at every stage.

Time allocated for liaison between all the child's teachers and his or her parents

Unfortunately, although the recommendations for identifying and assessing children with special needs in the Code of Practice are thorough and should help many pupils to be more effectively taught, they are time consuming. There is no suggestion where this extra time will come from. If additional money is allocated for the implementation of the Code it will be important that some of this is used to release special needs staff and subject teachers for vital liaison with each other for the good of the children's education.

There are SENCOs of large schools who are expected to fulfil these duties in about four non-contact periods a week, and share an office and telephone with five Heads of Year. I am sure they will be glad that it is stated, underneath these responsibilities:

> Governing bodies and headteachers may need to give careful thought to the SEN co-ordinator's timetable in the light of this Code and in the context of resources available in the school.

The link between learning difficulties, behavioural difficulties, and self-esteem

Throughout the section in the Code on special educational provision, there is a recognition of the link between learning and behavioural difficulties. An example of this is in para 3:5, when, after listing learning difficulties, it is stated:

> Some may also have poor social skills and may show signs of emotional and behavioural difficulties.

Again where clear recorded evidence of the child's learning difficulties is recommended (para 3:57) we find:

> There is evidence of significant emotional and behavioural difficulties, as indicated by clear recorded examples of withdrawn or

disruptive behaviour; a marked and persistent inability to concentrate; difficulties in establishing and maintaining balanced relationships with his or her fellow pupils or with adults; and any other evidence of significant delay in the development of life and social skills.

A similar paragraph (3:61) appears where specific learning difficulties (dyslexia) are examined.

However, throughout the Code these difficulties are not linked directly with self-esteem. Perhaps this is not surprising since this is a government document with recommendations for identifying and assessing measurable conditions. At the same time, the fact that the Code is clear about the importance of the child and the parents being listened to at each stage does indicate implicitly a greater awareness of how self-esteem is nurtured than is usual in official documents. Certainly the tone of the whole document is positive and recommends the monitoring and recognition of small steps of achievement, which is an important factor in relation to self-esteem.

The section in Stage 5 (6:59) on the statement review for young people aged 14–19 appears to have regard for self-esteem in recognising that:

effective arrangements for transition will involve young people themselves addressing issues of:
– personal development
– self-advocacy
– the development of a positive self image
– awareness of the implications of any long-term health problem or disability and
– the growth of personal autonomy and the acquisition of independent living skills.

A positive personality and philosophy on the part of the support teacher

The support teacher's role is clearly to be very involved in the IEPs and monitoring the child's progress. Para 2:110 urges the need for differentiation of work for many children and the importance of the teachers' ability to use a variety of materials and methods to address the child's difficulties. The special needs teacher's duties are defined and among the SENCO's duties is the responsibility for making sure that INSET in special needs is provided.

In order to work according to these new demands, with children whose needs have not differed greatly over the years it will be necessary for support teachers to be able to work in a positive way with their colleagues. At first, having responsibility for pupils who are on IEPs which are regularly monitored might put some stress on support teachers who have been more used to working in a reactive rather than proactive role. There will have to be an optimism and a generosity of spirit in order to offer to be a real help and support to the hard pressed teacher in the classroom who is being made more and more answerable for the education of every child in the room, however great the special need.

Compatibility between the subject and support teachers

There is no place in the Code for recommending that the subject and support teachers relate well to each other, although support arrangements can stand or fall on this issue. Making sure that the adults in the classroom are able to work together productively will be yet another task of the SENCO.

The appointment of a special needs co-ordinator for each faculty or subject area

Because of the different extent of the budgetary autonomy of schools, there are no specific recommendations of how learning support teams should be formed. In the secondary schools of which I have personal knowledge, the willingness of one volunteer in each department to learn as much as possible about special needs and be responsible for differentiation in his or her specialist subject, certainly seems to work well. Where the volunteers were teachers with no other special responsibility in the school, they seemed full of enthusiasm to do the job effectively. They showed evident enjoyment in talking about children's individual needs and were eager to share with me ideas they had for differentiation.

On an INSET day in one particular school I was briefing the entire staff and two of the governors on the implementation of the Code of Practice. I finished the day by asking the faculties to elect one of their members to lead the group and to go off and think of all the ways in which they could provide differentiation in their subject. They had half an hour to perform this task and the feedback took over an hour! There was a real sense of achievement as departments realised how, by sharing ideas, they could provide such a variety of methods. The spokesperson in each department took a pride in presenting the strategies which could often be adapted to use in other disciplines for the good of the pupils.

In secondary schools it is important that teachers in the same curriculum areas discuss special needs together. Although many of their means of differentiation are common to other subjects, some might be much more specific.

Availability of material resources for support

Some schools see the statement of special needs as a dowry. The money can be spent at the discretion of the headteacher, although the provision of a laptop computer, a tape recorder or another learning aid might be written into the statement. All schools also receive a sum of money for special needs in general. In some boroughs this is known as additional learning support (ALS) and it is traditionally calculated in relation to the proportion of the school population who are entitled to free or subsidised meals.

When headteachers in my investigation were asked how they spent this money, some explained that it was used to keep classes smaller throughout the school. Others explained that it meant that some lower stream classes, or some lower subject streams could be taught in smaller groups. In a few schools it was used entirely to buy equipment and to pay for teaching hours that would directly benefit all those children who were having difficulty with learning.

It will be interesting to see whether there will be any specification of how the money to be allocated to the schools for the implementation of the Code of Practice is to be spent. Although, in answer to a question at a conference in August 1994, the Secretary of State said that £24 million is to be given by the government for implementing the Code, it is not yet clear how it is to be distributed.

Availability of specialist advice for special educational needs

Specialist peripatetic teams who, because of the changing funding arrangements, suddenly found themselves having to market their services, were greatly relieved to see the recognition of their expertise in the Code of Practice. It will be important that these teams continue to be available to provide the expert input that will be required for pupils whose needs require the process to reach Stage 3, where the SEN co-ordinator continues to take a leading role, working closely with the child's teachers. The Code emphasises that the SENCO should be:

sharing responsibility for the child with external specialist services relevant to the child's needs. Such support will come from teachers in a learning or behavioural support service; peripatetic teachers, for example, teachers of the hearing or visually impaired; the education psychology service; child health and adolescent mental health services; social services; and advisors or teachers with knowledge of information technology for children with special educational needs. (para 2:101)

The Code goes on to recognise that the provision of these services is dependent on local policies which should be known to the SENCO. It also suggests that information on services can be obtained from the LEA and from NCET (National Council for Educational Technology).

INSET provision

It is good to see that one of the responsibilities of the SENCO is 'contributing to the in-service training of all staff'. (para 2:14) No longer is special needs training to be seen as an optional extra for those who have an interest in it. Since all staff will have in their classes children with special needs, all staff are to be given help in understanding these children. Section 2.26 is entitled 'The In-service training of staff' and is specific about the commitment that there must be within all schools:

The school's SEN policy should describe plans for the in-service training and professional development of staff to help them work effectively with pupils with special educational needs. The SEN in-service training policy should be part of the school's development plan and should, where appropriate, cover the needs of non-teaching assistants and other staff. Schools should consider the training needs of the SEN co-ordinator and how he or she can be equipped to provide training for fellow teachers. Schools and LEAs should also consider governing bodies' in-service training needs in the light of this Code. A school contemplating a particular special educational needs in-service training programme may wish to inform itself of the LEA's training policy and may also wish to consult other schools in the area with a view to securing economies of scale and sharing expertise.

The facility of withdrawal for a specific purpose

The Code does not attempt to specify how support is to be delivered, although it insists that there must be a plan for any child at Stage 2 or beyond, and the effectiveness of this support is to be monitored by regular meetings. Throughout the Code there is mention of professionalism, expertise and individual plans. If support teams are to be brought in to share the responsibility of the child's progress with the SENCO, these professionals together will be able to plan the best intervention. From experience related elsewhere in this book, we know that it is possible that this might best be achieved by withdrawing the child for individual work for a prearranged period as needed. I think the Code supports the second half of this statement where it is stressed that withdrawal support must be for a specific purpose.

Covert delivery of support for some secondary pupils

I am not sure how easy it will be to deliver covert support when there is an emphasis on planning the intervention for the individual carefully, and monitoring its effectiveness regularly. Perhaps the proof of this as a strategy will be when monitoring produces the evidence that the support delivered in this way has been effective.

I make no apology for including this strategy among indicators of effective support as this was mentioned time and time again by SENCOs. However, it was deliberately placed last since, as it depends on circumstances in the classroom beyond the control of the support teacher, it is clearly not the most effective method of delivering a targeted resource. At the time I was discussing support with SENCOs, we were focusing almost entirely on that given to the 2 per cent or 3 per cent of pupils who had been statemented. When the Code is implemented, and a greater number of unstatemented pupils have an IEP for at least part of their school career, pupils may well be less concerned about being seen to need help. It was already evident that those children who had come up from primary schools where they had been supported regularly in the classroom had no embarrassment about in-class support. Their only objection about being withdrawn from the room for help was that they would miss what was happening in the room.

How will the Code of Practice affect support in the secondary school classroom?

The publication of the Code of Practice for the Identification and Assessment of Special Educational Needs has given the pupils concerned and their teachers a higher profile. The days of children spending their entire secondary school careers in the remedial 'hut' are well and truly over. However with the raised profile comes an increased demand for accountability. It might no longer be sufficient to say that a pupil 'seems to be improving', or that 'he is gaining in confidence and self-esteem'. It will be necessary to be specific at review meetings and pin-point where the improvement has taken place and where the proof of improved self-esteem is and how this is being capitalised in nurturing the child's progress.

Since there will be a greater number of children whose work has to be differentiated and for whom a specific plan has to be made, there will be a need for support teachers who are both experienced in their work and have knowledge and expertise in the field of such special needs as specific learning difficulties and attention deficit disorder. Time will have to be allocated for liaison between teachers once pupils are working on IEPs.

Perhaps it is not too much to hope that the status of the support teacher will rise as special needs receives more attention from all staff in a school. There is a dilemma in this however, because, if all teachers in a school are to receive training in special needs, will the object of this be defeated by retaining special needs specialists within the classroom? Will some support teachers be replaced by a smaller number of peripatetic advisory teachers?

How will the Code of Practice serve the pupils with special educational needs?

By its thorough regard for planning and monitoring at frequent intervals, and by its insistence that information be shared by all those concerned with the child, resources should be used more effectively. It should remove some of the glaring anomalies that have occurred in neighbouring authorities at times.

The widening of the review meeting for statemented pupils, aged 14–19, to include those professionals who can help them to plan for the future, is a welcome innovation. In the past there has often been little attempt to plan for pupils with quite severe needs until a few weeks before the school leaving date.

Although the implementation of the Code is not statutory, any school not following its guidance will be expected to have a similar framework for special needs in place, if they are inspected by OFSTED. This means that the governors and senior management teams of schools will no longer be able to short change the most vulnerable and needy members of their communities. Perhaps this document will make the dreams of the keenest advocates of integration come true after a decade of struggling to make the ordinary school special.

APPENDIX 1

SCHOOL-BASED STAGES OF THE CODE OF PRACTICE

SCHOOL-BASED STAGES: STAGE 1

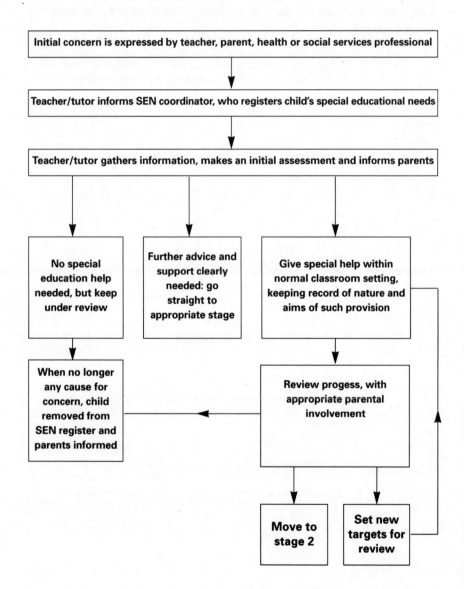

SCHOOL-BASED STAGES: STAGE 2

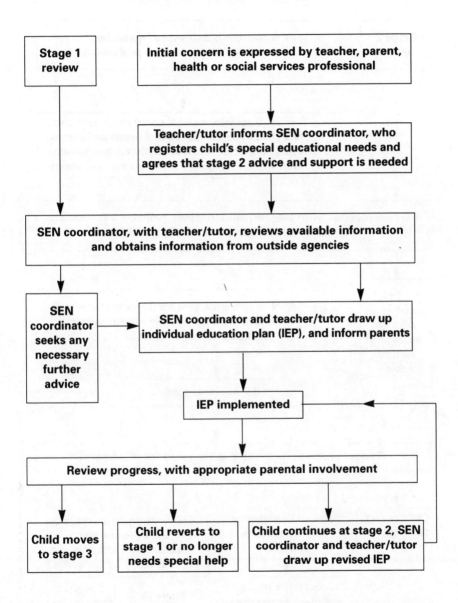

SCHOOL-BASED STAGES: STAGE 3

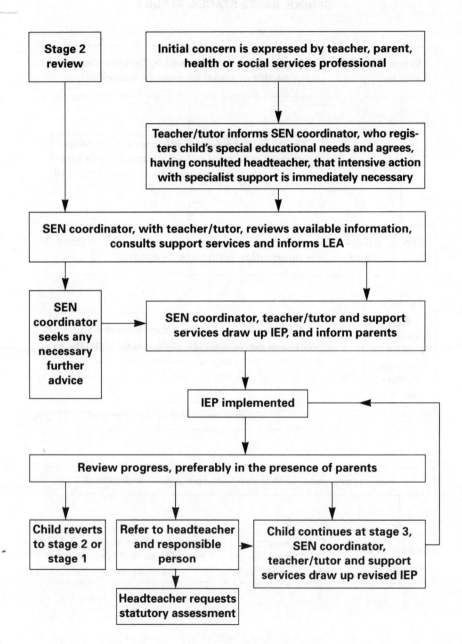

APPENDIX 2

Useful addresses for those concerned with adolescents with specific learning difficulties

British Dyslexia Association, 98 London Road, Reading RG1 5AU

Hornsby International Centre (Dyslexia), Glenshee Lodge, 261 Trinity Road, Wandsworth SW18 3SN *Tel:* 081 874 1844 (*Fax:* 081 877 9737)

Agencies and organisations for those concerned with adolescents with emotional and behavioural difficulties

AWCEBD, Charlton Court, East Sutton, Maidstone ME17 3DQ *Tel:* 0622 843104

The Association of Workers with Children with Emotionally and Behaviourally Difficulties (AWCEBD) has been in existence for many years. As the Association for Workers with Maladjusted Children it absorbed the Association for Therapeutic Education in the early 1980s. The journal of this Association is *Therapeutic Care and Education*. It contains book reviews and articles written by practitioners in the field of emotional and behavioural difficulty. These articles are based on current experience and research. The editing and selection of material for this journal is done by an academic committee and a high standard is maintained. They hold a study week during the Easter holiday each year and lectures and workshops during this week are usually given by some of the very well known names in this field. In recent years attendance at these weeks has been counted towards award bearing courses.

APSA, BMH Ltd, Norfolk House, Norfolk Way, Uckfield, East Sussex TN22 1EP *Tel:* 0825 760886

A useful organisation for secondary school teachers is APSA. This acronym originally stood for the Association for the Psychiatric Study of Adolescence but it was decided that this name alienated potential members without a medical background. The acronym has remained but now stands for the Association of Professionals in Services for Adolescents. The journal of this Association is *The Journal of Adolescence*. It is a learned journal which contains a few reports of fairly high powered research and is usually on a specific theme such as teenage pregnancy or self-mutilation. It is certainly worth having in a staff library. To celebrate the Association's twenty-fifth anniversary they have just introduced a new, 'light weight' journal called *Rapport* which contains easy to read articles about adolescent issues which have recently appeared in the press, reviews of books by and about adolescents and comments on services throughout the country. Their conference is usually during the first or second weekend of July and is an opportunity to hear international speakers on adolescent matters.

Young Minds, 22a Boston Place, London NW1 6ER *Tel:* 071 724 7262

This organisation has been formed by professionals who have been active in the other two organisations. It was formed as a reaction to the closure of many adolescent facilities during the early years of the nineties. Representatives from this organisation are often asked to state their views to the media when adolescent matters are at the forefront of the news. They produce an extremely interesting newsletter which is a fund of up-to-date information on both legislation and facilities for disturbed adolescents.

Contact with any of these organisations will result in information about local meetings and courses which they are holding. For support teachers who are members of small central teams, membership of these associations are an excellent way of acquiring a broader view of issues in this field.

Addresses for those concerned with hearing impaired pupils

National Deaf Children's Society, 45 Hereford Road, London W2 5AH

To promote public interest in and awareness of the needs of deaf children and their families, and to improve welfare and educational support. It provides information through its education officer and booklets on such topics as 'glue' ear and hearing aids. Its quarterly magazine is *Talk*.

British Association of Teachers of the Deaf, Service for the Hearing-Impaired, Icknield High School, Riddy Lane, Luton LU3 2AH

The professional association for teachers and others involved in the education of hearing impaired children; holds national and regional courses, conferences and meetings; promotes policy, research and training issues; publishes a range of technical, practical and theoretical articles in the *Journal of the British Association of Teachers of the Deaf.*

Addresses for those concerned with visually handicapped children

Royal National Institute for the Blind, 224 Great Portland Street, London W1N 6AA *Tel:* 071 388 1266.

(This is also the address on which to contact the Audio Reading Trust)

National Low Vision Advice Centre, 3 Colleton Crescent, Exeter EX2 4DG

Partially Sighted Society, Queen's Road, Doncaster DN1 2NX *Tel:* 0302 68998

SENSE (National Association for Deaf/Blind and Rubella Handicapped), 311 Grays Inn Road, London WC1 *Tel:* 071 278 1005

I have not included the addresses of all the firms which provide specialised equipment as these vary from time to time. However, all these organisations will be able to give advice on obtaining specialist aids.

Addresses for those interested in Thinking Skills

Centre For Thinking Skills, West London Institute, 300 St Margarets Road, Twickenham TW1 1PT
(3 information packs per year, annual fee £6)

To learn more about Instrumental Enrichment (Reuven Feuerstein) write to:

British Institute of Instrumental Enrichment, 53 Craigwell Avenue, Bognor Regis PO21 4XN *Tel:* 0243 825843

Thinking Skills Network, Mrs J. Robb, 36 Caldy Road, West Kirby L48 2HQ

(Journal *Multi Mind* plus information, annual fee £10)

References

Alsop, P. and McCaffrey, T. (eds) (1993) *How to Cope with Childhood Stress: Practical Guide for Teachers*. Harlow: Longman.

Audit Commission/HMI (1992) *Getting in on the Act: provision for pupils with special educational needs: the national picture*. London: DfE, HMSO.

Balshaw, M.H. (1993) *Help in the Classroom*. London: David Fulton Publishers.

Bell, P. and Best, R. (1986) *Supportive Education*. Oxford: Blackwell Education.

Best, R. (1991) 'Support Teaching in a Comprehensive School: Some reflections on recent experience', *Support for Learning*, **Vol.6**, No.1.

Beynon, J. (1985) *Initial Encounters in the Secondary School, Sussing, Typing and Coping*. London: Falmer Press.

Bibby, G. (1990) 'An evaluation of in-class support in a secondary school', *Support for Learning*, **Vol.5**, No.1.

Blagg, N., Ballinger, M. and Gardner, R. (1988) *Somerset Thinking Skills Course*. Oxford: Basil Blackwell.

Bloom, B.S. et al. (1956) *Taxonomy of Educational Goals: Handbook 1: Cognitive Domain*. New York: David McKay.

Bovair, K., Carpenter, B. and Upton, G. (1992) *Special Curricula Needs*. London: David Fulton Publishers.

Boxer, R. and Halpin, D. (1989) Planning for Support Teaching, in Evans, R. (ed) *Special Educational Needs: Policy into Practice*. Oxford: Blackwell Education.

Cardinal, D.N., Griffin, J.R. and Christenson, G.N. (1993) 'Do tinted lenses really help students with reading disabilities?' *Intervention in School and Clinic*, **Vol.24**, No.5.

Chapman, E.K. and Stone, J.M. (1988) *The Visually Handicapped Child in the Classroom*. London: Cassell Educational Ltd.

Charleton, T. and Hunt, J. (1993) 'Towards pupils' self-image enhancement: The EASI teaching programme', *Support for Learning*, **Vol.8**, No.3.

Connelly, M. and Friel, M. (1993) 'Miss, Are you a real teacher?', *Special* (the Bulletin of NASEN), February.

Cowne, E. and Norwich, B. (1987) *Lessons in Partnership: An Inset Course 'Meeting Special Educational Needs in Ordinary Schools'*. London: Institute of Education.

Davies, J.O. and Davies, P. (1988) 'Developing Credibility as a Support and Advisory Teacher', *Support for Learning*, **Vol.3**, No.1.

de Bono, E. (1970) *Lateral Thinking*. London: Ward Lock.

Department for Education (1989) *Discipline in Schools: Report of the Committee of Inquiry (The Elton Report)*. London: HMSO.

Department for Education (1994) *Code of Practice on the Identification and Assessment of Special Educational Needs*. London.

Department of Education and Science (1978) *Special Educational Needs (The Warnock Report)*. London: HMSO.

Dessent, T. (1987) *Making the Ordinary School Special*. London: Falmer Press.

Dodgeson, H. (1988) In-class Support: threat or challenge, in Evans, R. (ed) *Special Educational Needs: Policy into Practice*. Oxford: Blackwell Education.

Dyer, C. (1988) 'Which Support? An examination of the term', *Support for Learning*, **Vol.3**, No.1.

Dyson, A. (1992) 'Innovatory Mainstream Practice: what's happening in schools' provision for special educational needs?', *Support for Learning*, **Vol.7**, No.2.

Dyson, A. and Gaines, C. (eds) (1993) *Rethinking Special Needs in Ordinary Schools*. London: David Fulton Publishers.

Farnham-Diggory, S. (1978) *Learning Disabilities*. London: Fontana/Open Books.

Fergusson, N. and Adams, M. (1983) 'Assessing the Advantages of Team Teaching in Remedial Education: the remedial teacher's role', *Remedial Education*, **Vol.17**, No.1.

Feuerstein, R. (1978) *Just a minute...Let me think*. Baltimore, MD: University Park Press.

Feuerstein, R. (1980) *Instrumental Enrichment: an intervention program for cognitive modifiability*. Baltimore, MD: University Park Press.

Fisher, R. (1990) *Teaching Children to Think*. Hemel Hempstead: Simon and Schuster.

Gaines, C. (1993) 'Behaviour Support Goes Commercial', *Special* (the Bulletin of NASEN), June.

Hanko, G. (1985) *Supporting Special Needs in Ordinary Classrooms*. Oxford: Blackwell Education.

Hart, S. (1986) Evaluating Support Teaching, in Booth et al. (eds) *Curriculum for Diversity in Education*. Milton Keynes: Open University Press.

Haskell, S.H. and Barrett, E.K. (1989) (2nd edition) *The Education of Children with Motor and Neurological Disabilities*. London: Fetter and Hall.

Hawkridge, D. and Vincent, T. (1992) *Learning Difficulties and Computers: Access to the Curriculum*. London: Jessica Kingsley Publishers.

Irlen, H. (1991) *Reading by the Colours: Overcoming Dyslexia and other Reading Disabilities through the Irlen Method*. New York: Avery

138

Publishing Group.

Lacey, P. and Lomas, J. (1993) *Support Services and the Curriculum: A Practical Guide to Collaboration*. London: David Fulton Publishers.

Lennox, D. (1991) *See Me After School*. London: David Fulton Publishers.

Lipman, M., Sharp, A.M. and Oscanyon, F.S. (1980) *Philosophy in the Classroom*. Philadelphia: Temple University Press.

Lovey, J. (1992) *Teaching Troubled and Troublesome Adolescents*. London: David Fulton Publishers.

Lovey, J. (1993) Defining Effective Statement Support, Unpublished MA dissertation, Roehampton Institute (University of Surrey).

MacConville, R. (1991) A Support Services Response to the 1988 Act, in Bowers, T. *Management Issues in the Wake of LMS*. Cambridge: Perspective Press.

Mason, M. (1992) The Integration Alliance, background and manifesto, in Booth et al. *Policies for Diversity in Education*. Milton Keynes: Open University Press.

Morrison, F.J., Giordani, B. and Nagy, J. (1977) 'Reading Disability; an information processing analysis', *Science,* **196**, 4285.

Moses, D., Hegarty, S. and Jowett, S. (1988) *Supporting Ordinary Schools: LEA Initiatives*. Windsor: NFER–Nelson.

O'Hanlon, C. (1993) *Special Education Integration in Europe*. London: David Fulton Publishers.

Ramasut, A. (1990) *Support for Special Needs in the Secondary School*. Lewes: Falmer Press.

Robertson, J. (1981) *Effective Classroom Control*. London: Hodder and Stoughton.

Slade, M. (1990) *One Step at a Time*. Wrexham: Maysdale Books.

Slee, R. (1993) *Is There a Desk With My Name On It? The Politics of Integration*. London: Falmer Press.

Stirling, E.G. (1985) *Help for the Dyslexic Adolescent*. Llandudno, Gwynedd: St David's College.

Swan, W. (1984) *Statistics of Segregation*. Childright No. 8.

Tansley, P. and Panckhurst, J. (1981) *Children with Specific Learning Difficulties*. Windsor: NFER-Nelson.

Thomas, G. (1992) 'Evaluating Support', *Support for Learning*, **Vol.5**, No.1.

Thomas, G. (1992) *Effective Classroom Teamwork – support or intrusion?* London: Falmer Press.

Vulliamy, G. and Webb, R. (1992) *Teacher Research and Special Educational Needs*. London: David Fulton Publishers.

Also see adult dyslexia book?

Index

140